JANE JACOBS
The Nature of Economies

Jane Jacobs was born in Scranton, Pennsylvania, and since 1968 has lived in Toronto, where she has taken an active role in helping to shape the city. Her previous books include *The Death and Life of Great American Cities* (1961), *The Economy of Cities* (1968), *The Question of Separatism* (1980), *Cities and the Wealth of Nations* (1984), *Systems of Survival* (1993), and *A Schoolteacher in Old Alaska* (1996).

ALSO BY JANE JACOBS

The Death and Life of Great American Cities

The Economy of Cities

The Question of Separatism

Cities and the Wealth of Nations

Systems of Survival

A Schoolteacher in Old Alaska (editor)

The Nature
of Economies

The
Nature
of
Economies

JANE JACOBS

VINTAGE BOOKS
A Division of Random House, Inc.
New York

FIRST VINTAGE BOOKS EDITION, MARCH 2001

The Library of Congress has cataloged the Modern Library edition as follows:
Jacobs, Jane.
The nature of economies / Jane Jacobs.
p. cm.
Includes index.
1. Economics—Environmental aspects. I. Title.
HD75.6.J325 2000
330—dc21 99-41014

Vintage ISBN: 0-375-70243-1

www.vintagebooks.com

Printed in the United States of America
10 9 8 7 6 5

For Burgin, Ned, and Jim

Foreword

Theories and other abstractions are powerful tools only in the limited sense that the Greek mythological giant Antaeus was powerful. When Antaeus was not in intimate contact with earth, his strength rapidly ebbed. The aim of the talkative characters in this book is to bring rarefied economic abstractions into contact with earthy realities, meaning universal natural processes of development, growth, and stability that govern economic life.

The theme running throughout this exposition—indeed, the basic premise on which the book is constructed—is that human beings exist wholly within nature as part of natural order in every respect. To accept this unity seems to be difficult for those ecologists who assume—as many do, in understandable anger and despair—that the human species is an interloper in the natural order of things. Neither is this unity easily accepted by economists, industrialists, politicians, and others who assume—as many do, taking understandable pride in human achievements—that reason, knowledge, and determination make it possible for human beings to circumvent and outdo the natural order. Readers unwilling or unable to breach a barrier that they imagine separates humankind and its works from the rest of nature will be unable to hear what this book is saying.

In describing natural processes and selecting examples to illustrate them, I have hewed to information from the fields of biology, evolutionary theory, ecology, geology, meteorology, and other natural sciences as the information is currently understood and interpreted by practitioners in these sciences. When, on infrequent occasions, my characters introduce their own interpretations of natural science, they make it clear that these are their own speculations. On economics they are much more opinionated in their insistence that it come down to earth, but again they state outrightly when they are being iconoclastic, and why.

I have used imaginary characters and didactic dialogue primarily because this venerable literary form is suited to expounding inquiry and developing argument, but also because the form implicitly invites a reader to join the characters and enter the argument too. A book is equipped to speak for itself, more so than any other artifact. But to be heard, a book needs a collaborator: a reader with a sufficiently open mind to take in what the book is saying and dispute or agree, but in any case think about it. Insofar as that process is enjoyably interesting as well as possibly useful—as I hope it may be—so much the better.

JANE JACOBS
Toronto, July 1999

Contents

Contents

The Nature
of Economies

Chapter 1

DAMN, ANOTHER ECOLOGIST

"Hortense and Ben have broken up," said Armbruster, waving a fax at Kate as she slid into the booth, balancing her cup of coffee.

"I'm sorry but not surprised," said Kate. "Remember how Ben used to gloat over industrial disasters? He thought everything industrial or technological was unnatural and that everything unnatural was bad."

"He meant well," Armbruster said. "We need Jeremiahs, but it must have been depressing for Hortense to live with one. It seems the breakup happened some time ago and she's gotten over it. She's interested in a new man. Mind if I finish this fax? I only got it as I was leaving the house."

In late morning they were sitting in an almost-empty coffee shop on lower Fifth Avenue, not far from Armbruster's Gramercy Square apartment. It was an unappealing restaurant in a stretch of New York rapidly going upscale. Armbruster liked it as his morning hangout because its well-deserved unpopularity guaranteed seats for acquaintances dropping by. He lived alone, and since his retirement from a small book publishing company, he missed his work and its daily give-and-take with colleagues.

"Damn, Hortense has found another ecologist," Armbruster grumbled as he continued reading the fax.

"That's not surprising, either," said Kate. "She's an environmental lawyer, so those are the people she talks to, consorts with. Those and other lawyers."

"But listen to this: His name is Hiram Murray IV. The Fourth! What an affectation."

"He's not to blame if his family ran out of names."

"You drop off the numbers when they die. I dropped off my Junior when my father died. Only kings and popes hang on to numbers."

"Maybe the other three are still alive—you don't know."

"Let's see," Armbruster mused aloud. "Number two would be his grandfather, and number one—" His eyes widened, exaggerating his customary owlish expression. "Good heavens, Hortense is fifty. You don't suppose—"

"No, I don't think Hortense is running around with a kid. Read on."

"Well, well, she's planning to come back from California," Armbruster read on. "He has a house in Hoboken. What's an ecologist doing in Hoboken? She says I'll like him and she's bringing him over a week from Thursday unless she hears otherwise, and so on."

"May I come too?" Kate asked. "It'll be wonderful to see Hortense again. And remember, Armbruster, I'm a fringe ecologist myself."

When Kate was denied tenure a few years previously in the biology department of the Long Island university where she taught and did neurobiological research, she found a job on a prospering science newsweekly, partly on the strength of her editing experience on *Systems of Sur-*

vival, a dialogue she and Armbruster had put together from conversations and reports by a little group Armbruster had got up to explore the different moral systems appropriate to different kinds of workers—such as police, legislators, clergy, and others holding positions of public trust, on the one hand, and manufacturers, bankers, merchants, and others in commercial pursuits, on the other. Hortense, who was Armbruster's niece, had been one of the group. During her first several months in her unfamiliar work on the weekly, Kate had frequently asked Armbruster for help and advice with her editing. After she no longer needed his guidance, she continued to drop in on him from time to time out of friendship.

A week from the following Thursday, at Armbruster's small apartment—crowded with books and signed photographs of authors on walls and tabletops—Hortense and Kate greeted each other affectionately and Hortense introduced Hiram. At tedious faculty meetings, Kate had learned to pass the time by imagining childhood versions of her colleagues' faces. Now, in Hiram, she saw a well-brought-up, thin-faced, eager boy grown into a good tweed suit and a receding hairline, his eagerness still intact.

As Hortense sat down on the sofa, Hiram remained standing, distractedly patting his jacket pockets. Kate glanced around the room in puzzlement. "Did you lose something, or mislay it?" she asked him.

"No, why—oh." He dropped his hands and smiled sheepishly. "I quit smoking five weeks and four days ago, and I still keep hunting for a cigarette." Hortense, Armbruster, and Kate, reformed smokers all, smiled sympathetically and Hortense patted his hand as he sat down beside her.

Knowing that Armbruster would be itching to deal with

Hiram's dynastic pretensions, as soon as they were settled with drinks Kate remarked offhandedly to Hiram, "That Four after your name is unusual. Not unheard-of, of course, but unusual."

Hiram made room between a book and a photograph on an end table and set down his drink. "My father's a splendid old man, but he insists on being Three, so I have to be Four. He's an economist and he would've liked me to be an economist, too, but after a try I dropped it for environmental studies. Most people I knew—this was thirty years ago—thought that it was like majoring in canoeing or birdwatching, but Pop took what I was doing seriously. I just mention this to show how minor his crotchet about the numbers is. 'Live and let live' runs both ways. But I did draw a line. My own son is named Joel."

"What do you do as an ecologist?" asked Armbruster. "Rally people around to save the woods and punish polluters?" Hortense and Kate exchanged glances, as if to acknowledge Armbruster's implicit, not very kindly, reference to Ben.

"No, although saving forests and reducing pollution are important. I'm a fund-raiser and facilitator. Specifically, I give organizational advice and help find grants for people—scientists—most of whom are trying to develop products and production methods learned from nature. Biomimicry, that approach is called. There's a book about it by that name. I'll get you a copy if you're interested. Two copies," he added, turning to Kate.

"Oh, I have it. I reviewed it," said Kate. "It's a good book, Armbruster. Broadly speaking, the aims are to make better materials than we manufacture now, but to make them at life-friendly temperatures and without toxic ingredients, like the filaments spiders make or the shell material abalones construct, for instance. Ideally, by imitating the chemistry of nature, we should be able to make materials and products by methods that are benign and, at the end of their lives as products, return them to earth or sea to degrade benignly."

"So many other possibilities are being explored," said Hortense. "Think of the energy, soil, artificial fertilizer, and chemicals such as weed killers that could be saved if grain fields didn't require annual plowing or planting—if wheat or rye could grow like perennial grasses in prairies. All green plants capture sunlight, but it's a puzzle and wonder how duckweed captures sunlight so effectively and uses it so efficiently. That's worth learning from. You get the idea, Armbruster?"

"Interesting," Armbruster replied, "but it sounds like just another way for us to exploit nature—trying to get out of technological messes with more technological messes."

Kate suppressed a snicker at Armbruster's mischievous adoption of Ben's persona and glanced at Hortense to catch her reaction. Hortense, who usually remained cool and elegant under provocation, uncharacteristically bristled. "No! This isn't exploiting nature! It's learning from nature, with the object of undoing damage and getting along with nature more harmoniously. Biomimics are the last people deserving thoughtless dismissal, Armbruster. You have no idea how difficult these puzzles are, how hard and complicated it is to learn the way prairies manage to replenish themselves year after year. What's gotten into you? You didn't use to be so negative and glib. You sound like Ben!"

"Just curious. You've put me in my place. But if these endeavors are so difficult, they may not be practical."

When neither Hortense nor Kate replied, Hiram spoke

up again, rubbing his forehead thoughtfully. "Biomimicry is a form of economic development. So caring about biomimicry requires caring about economic development—hoping it continues vigorously. Otherwise, we can't hope for better products and safer methods. How else can we get them? Thinking about development has made me realize how similar economies and ecosystems are. That's to say, principles at work in the two are identical. I don't expect you to believe this just because I say so, but I'm convinced that universal natural principles limit what we can do economically and how we can do it. Trying to evade overriding principles of development is economically futile. But those principles are solid foundations for economies. My personal biomimicry project is to learn economics from nature."

"Bravo!" said Armbruster, sensing a book in the making. His eyes shifted to the tape recorder on a shelf.

"Uh-uh, Armbruster," said Hortense. "No symposium; no reports. Not again. Can't we have a conversation without that recorder? Can't we just talk? Can't you forget about trying to produce a book? There are so many other interesting things you could do, now that you have time." Kate caught Hortense's eye and, waggling her eyebrows, signaled to Hortense to pipe down.

"Producing a book never crossed my mind," Armbruster lied. "But it did cross my mind that I'd like a tape. Economic development interests me, too. What harm?"

"I don't mind if Kate and Hortense don't," said Hiram. He finished the last of his drink and set down his glass, with a questioning smile directed first to Hortense, then to Kate.

Hortense shrugged and Kate grinned while Armbruster moved his machine to the coffee table, pushed the record button, nodded to Hiram, and said, "What did you mean about learning economics from nature? Economies are human, not natural. They're artificial, with the possible exception of primitive foraging."

"A common assumption, and one can see why," said Hiram. "After all, only human beings employ smart, educated border collies to herd sheep. Only human beings build hospitals and operate on cleft palates, or wrap snacks in plastic, or issue credit cards and send monthly bills. We differ from other creatures in the ways we make our living, but different doesn't necessarily mean artificial. We don't call bees' activities artificial because they manufacture honey, nor beavers' because they log and build dams, nor seahorses' because the males hatch and nurture the young. We don't call sunflowers artificial because they're so much taller than daisies. Our own manual dexterity and brains are created by nature. What we can do with those assets comes to us as naturally as the ability to spin webs and to sting netted prey comes to spiders."

"Not so fast," said Armbruster. "I didn't mean we're biologically artificial but that we create artificial things and impose them on the world of nature. We make artificial leather, artificial turf for stadiums, artificial teeth, artificial ice, and so on. How can you say human beings don't have artificial economies?"

"Armbruster, that's like accusing spiders of artificiality because they're spinning something other than cotton, flax, silk, wool, or hemp fibers," said Kate. "Please relax and let's listen before we argue."

"If we stop focusing on *things*," said Hiram, "and shift attention to the processes that generate the things, distinctions between nature and economy blur. That's not a new idea. Early ecologists were quick to see—"

"Who were the early ecologists?" asked Armbruster.

"Botanists who became interested in plant communities—groups of plant species whose interdependence seemed so similar to economic relationships that the naturalists coined a new word for natural communities of organisms and based it directly on the word *economy*. That was late in the nineteenth century."

"Wait!" said Armbruster, darting to his unabridged dictionary. "Aha, *economy* is derived from two Greek roots—*oiko*, meaning 'house,' and *nomy*, meaning 'management': house management. *Ecology* comes from the same root for 'house,' plus the root *logy* for 'logic' or 'knowledge.' So *ecology* literally means 'house knowledge.' Now, that's strange, isn't it? *Bio*, meaning 'life,' and *nomy*, 'management'—*bionomy*, 'life management,' would have been more to the point. Victorian scholars were well grounded in Greek. Odd that they embraced jargon as imprecise as *ecology*."

"Not odd when you realize they thought of ecology as 'the economy of nature,'" said Hiram, "a definition still in currency. The very sound of their new word tagged it as the twin of *economy*. That was their point, regardless of literal meaning. They were studying the economy of nature. I'm studying the nature of economy. Same affinity, glimpsed from an opposite angle.

"Natural processes obviously aren't founded on human behavior," Hiram continued. "Instead, nature affords foundations for human life and sets its possibilities and limits. Economists seem not to have grasped this reality yet. But many people engaged in various economic activities do realize it's important to learn from nature and apply the knowledge to what they do. For instance, modern metallurgists can observe the changes that take place in lattices of metallic crystals owing to temperature variations and alloy combinations—information old smiths had no access to, because they didn't have X-ray crystallography. Architects and engineers accept the reality of natural forces of tension and compression and the help of tables of properties of construction materials. Wine makers, cheese makers, and bakers grasp and value their cooperative relationships with yeasts and bacteria; sanitary engineers, physicians, and organic farmers have learned to do the same and are still learning.

"In sum," he went on, "all kinds of people now understand that their success depends on working knowledgeably along with natural processes and principles, and respecting those processes and principles. That's very different from supposing that success depends on lore handed down from supernatural sources or on blind trial and error—and diametrically different from supposing that human beings are exempt from nature's dictates or that they are masters of nature.

"To repeat, I'm convinced that economic life is ruled by processes and principles we didn't invent and can't transcend, whether we like that or not, and that the more we learn of these processes and the better we respect them, the better our economies will get along."

"That sounds pretty pessimistic," said Armbruster. "Here we are, already loaded up with government regulations. And now you want to compile still more lists of economic rules and regulations decreed by nature?"

"Limits are part of it," replied Hiram. "Awareness of them can prevent futility. Alchemists did better after they gave up trying to turn base metals into gold and to discover a universal solvent and instead applied themselves to studying chemistry. But here's what interests me most: Natural principles of chemistry, mechanics, and biology are not merely limits. They're invitations to work along with them.

"I think it's the same with economics. Working along with natural principles of development, expansion, sustainability, and correction, people can create economies that are more reliably prosperous than those we have now and that are also more harmonious with the rest of nature."

"I'm glad to hear you say 'the rest of nature,' " said Kate. "If it's actually true that natural processes rule human economic life—or could if we'd let them—it follows that we're an integral part of the natural world instead of its mere disturbers and destroyers."

"That's not necessarily a reassuring thought," said Hortense. "Plenty of other animal species have naturally gone extinct, along with their practices, whatever they were—you know that, Kate. Nothing is more unforgiving of error than nature. If we poison our own water and air with hormone-mimicking chemicals that we don't understand, it isn't reassuring to realize that nature's solution for maladaptations is extinction."

Armbruster cut short the potentially interesting point Hortense had raised. "Before we move on to anything else," he said, "I'd like to mention a few subjects that I consider economic fundamentals. You haven't said one word about money. But economics is first and foremost about money. What does nature say about money?"

"Nature says money is a feedback-carrying medium," Hiram replied. "Money is useful to economic self-regulation in the process we've come to call negative-feedback control. But the usefulness of money is far from enough to explain how economies work."

"What about the law of diminishing returns?" asked Armbruster. "First you cream off what's easiest and cheapest to exploit, then getting more is increasingly hard and expensive. That's certainly fundamental to economic life."

"The law of diminishing returns is truthful and harsh," said Hiram, "but it explains little about economic life in the absence of the converse law, which we might call the law of responsive substitution, meaning that people seek or contrive substitutes for resources that have become too expensive. Obvious examples have been domesticated animals in place of wild game; petroleum in place of whale oil and, later, coal; plastics in place of tortoiseshell and ivory. But that raises questions about development which demand some analysis of development in the rest of nature."

"What are you going to do with your project of economic biomimicry?" asked Armbruster.

"Write a book, I suppose," said Hiram. "Or put it on the Web. Or make practical use of it, advising clients. But that's premature. I've only partly formulated it. This isn't my work, just my hobby, a sideline. My main work is finding funds to keep other biomimics going—even though they're a frugal lot."

"I don't want to pry," said Armbruster, "but what do you live on? Commissions from grants you help to find?"

"No, I get paid for my time as a consultant. And I do some lecturing. Fortunately, I inherited my Hoboken house from my mother. It's enough room for my office and two apartments that I rent out, as well as my own apartment. I drifted into consulting after my father and I provided a little capital to a group in New Jersey working with novel and promising ways of treating sewage. I soon saw that development work of that sort needed more research and experimental capital than we could dream of affording, so I began hunting for more and turned out to be good at it. You could say I found a niche in the environment. I can't imagine doing anything more interesting, because of the amazing people and ideas I get involved with, but it doesn't leave me much uninterrupted time."

"Which reminds me how late it is," said Hortense, rising.

"Wait," said Armbruster. "All you've told us is why you think learning economics from nature isn't outlandish. You haven't told us what you've learned. Can't you go a bit further?"

"Better not tonight. But we can arrange a time for me to bring you that book I promised and to talk some more." As Kate, Hortense, and Hiram were putting on their coats, Armbruster jubilantly stuck a Post-it note on his refrigerator door, reminding himself to stock up on blank cassettes.

Chapter 2

THE NATURE OF DEVELOPMENT

"Start where you like. I've no idea what to ask you," said Armbruster two weeks later as he switched on his recorder at the next session with Hiram, Hortense, and Kate.

"I'd like to start with development," said Hiram. "Where do new things come from? Why doesn't everything stay as it previously was? Let's define development as significant qualitative change, usually building up incrementally. But even single instances of qualitative change can be significant—for instance, resistance to specific antibiotics developed by some strains of bacteria."

"Oh, I thought you were going to talk about economic development," said Armbruster, his enthusiasm fading into disappointment.

"I am, but first come fundamentals applying to all development."

"Does that include inanimate development?" asked Kate.

"How can there be inanimate development?" Hortense protested.

"Think a minute," said Kate. "Rivers develop deltas by depositing silt. Waves develop sandbars. Volcanic eruptions develop mountains. Weather systems develop fronts and storms—"

"Let Hiram proceed," said Armbruster. "Otherwise we'll never get to economic development."

"Means of development vary enormously," Hiram continued, "as Kate has just indicated. A rabbit embryo and a bean sprout don't develop by exactly the same means, even though they're both alive. Yet an animal, a plant, a delta, a legal code, or an improved shoe sole—they all depend on the same underlying process for development."

"Don't expect me to take that outrageous statement on faith," said Armbruster. "You must mean it metaphorically."

"No, I'm not dealing in metaphors. Nineteenth-century embryologists and evolutionists were the first to try seriously to understand the development of one form from another as a natural process. The gist of their definitions of development was this: *differentiation emerging from generality.* Only four words—but they describe development on every scale of time and size, whether animate or inanimate.

"To take an example on a huge scale, consider the solar system. According to astronomers and physicists, it seems once to have been a vast cloud of matter. That was a generality. Differentiations emerged: the sun, fellow planets and their moons, along with various smaller debris and leftover generalized matter.

"Now, the next important point: Once the earth emerged as a differentiation, it became a new generality from which further differentiations could emerge. From the crust, in due course, emerged the kinds of differentiations Kate mentioned. So here's the second universal principle of development: *Differentiations become generalities from which further differentiations emerge.* In other words, development is an open-ended process, which creates complexity and diversity, because multiplied generalities are sources of multiplied differentiations—some occurring simultaneously in parallel, others in successions. Thus a simple basic process, when repeated and repeated and repeated, produces staggering diversity.

"On a tiny scale—say, an embryonic human being—the generality is a microscopically small fertilized egg. At first it divides into repetitions of itself, forming a blob of multiplied generality. The first differentiations to emerge, depending on their locations in the blob, are layers of three distinctly differentiated kinds of cells, called ectoderm, mesoderm, and endoderm. These three differentiations are also three new generalities, from which more and more differentiations can emerge, both simultaneously and in successions, producing the diverse and complicated tissues and organs of the developing baby. In the infant's reproductive organ, a preserve of undifferentiated eggs or sperm is set aside for producing the next generation's differentiations."

"But babies aren't a new thing," said Hortense. "They're a multiplication of what already exists."

"To be sure, in one sense," Hiram replied. "But in another sense, each is a unique individual. In either sense, each new one emerges by the process I've sketched. Evolutionists, of course, were concerned not just with individuals but with how the species itself emerged—and all other species, living and extinct. They worked out long progressions of lineages—that is, sequential generalities and differentiations. The diverging sequences are conventionally depicted as a tree or bush of life, with human beings on a topmost twig of the mammal branch on the tree.

"Sequences of more limited scope are conventionally depicted in linear, comic-strip fashion, such as the development of the horse from a smallish, fully-toed, nondescript quadruped to a magnificent hoofed steed. Or, to take an even narrower example, the various kinds of mammalian feet were differentiated from unspecialized feet of early mammals, which had five generalized toes with claws, apparently much like the unspecialized feet of modern rats.

"Differentiations that emerged from those ratlike feet included hooves of horses, wings of bats, flippers of whales, paws of cats, and our own hands, which happen to be closer to the unspecialized early mammal feet than those others. In our case, the significant digital development—not nearly as spectacular or specialized as hooves, flippers, or bat wings—was our opposable thumbs, which permit our superb manual dexterity."

"All you've told us so far, if you'll pardon me, is obvious to the point of banality," said Armbruster. "How else could differentiations emerge except from prior generalities?"

"My point exactly," said Hiram. "While this is obvious to you, it was not obvious to anybody until fairly recently. Aristotle, and other learned men long after him, thought a human embryo began as a minuscule infant that grew larger and stronger in the womb. And even today many people can't credit evolution, preferring to believe that the world and its creatures were preformed from the start, as stated in Genesis."

"Those evolutionary graphics," said Kate. "They're useful for identifying lineages, but they're incomplete and misleading. A horse requires more than its own ancestors. A horse implies grass. Grass implies topsoil. Topsoil implies breakup of rocks, development of fungi, worms, beetles, compost-making bacteria, animal droppings—no end of other evolution and lineages besides that of the horse."

"Yes, I was coming to that next," said Hiram. "It's the last of three fundamental development principles: *Development depends on co-developments*. I mean that development can't usefully be thought of as a 'line,' or even as a collection of open-ended lines. It operates as a web of interdependent co-developments. No co-development web, no development."

"Aren't you and Kate talking about this process only when it gets pretty far along?" asked Armbruster. "When it's already very complicated? There surely had to be development without co-development before things became so complicated and webby."

"Co-developments may always have been necessary to the process of differentiation," Hiram replied. "Consider that the earth is not in the solar system by itself."

"Okay, the planets need the sun or they couldn't hold to orbits. But how does something like a delta need co-development?" asked Armbruster.

"A delta needs both water and grit. Neither, by itself, can develop a delta and each by itself is a result of co-developments," Hiram answered.

"As a practical matter, development doesn't occur in isolation. Every animal cell, including each of our own cells, of course, carries within it descendants of bacteria called mitochondria, which have their own lineage, different from that of the cell in which they live. Mitochondria have their own genetic material—they evolved separately—but now they and our cells are symbionts, mutually dependent, although originally they may have co-developed as predators and prey.

"Mitochondria power our cells—generate energy—by combining sugar and oxygen; to oversimplify, mitochondria feed the flame of animal life by burning sugar. Cells of green plants benefit from co-developed symbionts called chloroplasts, which capture sunlight and use it as energy to free carbon—the basic food of plants—from carbon dioxide."

"The waste product of chloroplasts is oxygen, which animals require," said Kate. "The waste product of mitochondria is carbon dioxide, which plants require. Neither plants nor animals would have a feasible atmosphere to draw on or live in without the other."

"Of course, Armbruster, co-development webs have become increasingly intricate as development has proceeded," said Hiram. "But we've every reason to believe that mutually influential co-developments are as old as development. In their growing intricacy, they come to incorporate all degrees of cooperation—"

"Now you *are* drifting into metaphor," said Armbruster. "Cooperation implies conscious intent. Can you properly speak of cooperation among plants or animals that don't know they're cooperating? When it's just the way things are for them?"

"That's a blurry line," said Hortense. "An ecologist in Oregon, back home from Botswana, told me about the honey bird, a drab little thing notable for being able to digest beeswax. It can't get at honey or wax by itself, because it would be stung to death. So it enlists human help by getting the attention of a hunter and leading him to a hive. The hunter overcomes the bees with a smudge fire, breaks open the hive, and shares the goodies with the bird."

"I'll grant that as cooperation," said Armbruster, "because the hunter knows he's cooperating."

"Ah," Hortense replied, "but the honey bird has one other species of helpers: small, skunklike mammals. Naturalists suppose these were the bird's traditional helpers. Same routine: The bird gets the attention of one of these creatures, leads it on, the animal backs up to the hive, sprays it with his powerful odor, breaks into the hive, and shares its goodies with the bird. If using a smoke smudge is cooperative behavior, why isn't using a stink smudge?"

Before Armbruster could answer, Hiram admitted, "*Cooperation* was a poorly chosen word. Even among human neighbors, where cooperation indisputably exists, it can be inadvertent. My tenant told me he misses me when I'm out of town because he depends on hearing my morning alarm clock—inadvertent cooperation on my part. The world's full of it. From now on, I'll just speak of interdependence, leaving aside whether it's intended or not."

"All this co-development, cooperation, symbiosis, interdependence," grumbled Armbruster. "The three of you make nature sound like a barn raising, everybody pitching in together. Where's the fierce competition? Where's the nature red in tooth and claw? Where's survival of the fittest and devil take the hindmost?"

"Oh, competition's there, and so are winners and losers," said Hiram. "Losers die and winners eat. The honey bird, skunklike mammal and hunter in Hortense's example are predators and the hive is prey. But that's not the whole cast of characters. The bees and their honey wouldn't exist without flowers, but the flowers wouldn't exist without bees; and so on. Put it this way: Competitions for feeding and breeding take place in an arena. The arena is a habitat. The fittest panther in the jungle is a goner if its habitat goes. And what is a habitat? It's an intricate, complicated web of interdependencies."

"An economy consists of interdependent relationships, competing and yet also knitting together co-developments," said Armbruster. "I agree with all that. Haven't you prepared us sufficiently to discuss economic development?"

"Yes," Hiram answered, "but first I'll remind you of the universal principles. Development is differentiation emerging from generality. A given differentiation is a new generality, from which further differentiations can potentially emerge. Thus the process is open-ended and it produces increasing diversity and increasingly various, numerous, and intricate co-development relationships. All this is the consequence of one simple sort of event repeated, repeated, repeated, and repeated."

"You've just identified a fractal," said Kate.

"I keep coming across references to fractals," said Hortense, "but what are they? And why should we care about them?"

"They're complicated-looking patterns that are actually made up of the same motif repeated on different scales," said Kate. "For instance, a muscle is a twisted bundle of fibers. Dissect out any one of those fiber bundles, and you find that it, too, is a twisted bundle of fibers. And so on. When you get down to the irreducibly smallest fiber, which you need an electron microscope to see, you find that it's a twisted strand of molecules. That's a real-life fractal. Mathematicians make computer-generated fractals, fascinating in their complexity and seeming variety, yet each fractal is made of repetitions."

"We should care about fractals," said Hiram, "because lots of things that seem impossible to comprehend become more understandable if we identify the basic pattern and watch what it produces through repetition. It's a way of dealing with some complexities that otherwise are impenetrable—the way development as we've described it was impenetrable to Aristotle.

"Of course, development still embodies mystery. Why should there be a force driving the universe toward intricacy and away from simplicity? But if the *why* of development is impenetrable, at least the *how* of development is discernible, and this has practical value, not least for economic development—"

"At last!" said Armbruster. "Wait till I change the cassette."

"Economic development displays the same pattern as any other development," Hiram resumed after their drinks were refreshed and Hortense, rummaging in the kitchen, had produced a tray of crackers and cheese. "This is most obvious when the differentiations happen to be new varieties of animals or plants."

"Oh, please, let's not get diverted back to nature," said Armbruster.

"We're in economic life now," said Hiram, "specifically, agriculture and animal husbandry. Human beings have deliberately developed hundreds of new varieties—although not new species—of dogs, pigs, goats, and other animals, along with thousands of new varieties—and some new species—of edible and ornamental plants. They've done this by fostering desirable differentiations and selecting those worth further fostering. Have you ever tasted a wild orange? Awful, though beautiful. One of my clients has been developing cotton with color differences. No dye required.

"Our remote ancestors started developing tools and weapons with nothing that was of their own making. They began with found generalities—already provided by development in the rest of nature: sticks, stones, bones, fire. They differentiated those found generalities into hammers, spears, scrapers, pokers, and torches, and, as one development led to another, into bows, arrowheads, nets, rafts, pigments, trumpets, cloaks, bags, and so on. The more differentiations, the more generalities; and the more generalities, the more bases for further developments, and so on.

"Because that's the universal development process, economic developments don't come out of thin air. They have lineages and pedigrees, the same as other forms of natural development. Consider the wheel family, for instance. We can't be sure of the ancestral generality from which the first wheel emerged, because that happened so far back in prehistory—"

"We can make a pretty good guess," Kate interrupted. "The oldest known cartwheels were wood, and solid instead of spoked, so it's reasonable to suppose the wheel's ancestor was an ordinary log used as a roller beneath loads. The differentiation would have been a cross-section of a log penetrated by a central axle."

"Maybe," said Hortense, "but I think a toy is more plausible. I visualize small solid circles—say, slices of gingerroot or squash—that mothers twirled on sticks to amuse themselves and the children. It's easier to slice a fruit or vegetable than a log. Kids who played with twirlers punched onto sticks might grow up to invent wheels."

"In that case, the generality would have been a flimsy little thing," said Hiram. "The significant differentiation would have been a bigger copy in sturdier material. Could be. Lots of developments have begun as ornaments or amusements. The first railroad was a London amusement ride, developed specifically for that purpose.

"Let's pretend we have an evolutionary tree of the wheel. Its root would be a rolling object of some kind, wood or other vegetable, yielding the differentiation of a solid wooden wheel. Branching off from it would be a lighter, stronger, and spoked wheel. In its turn, that would be a new generality, the progenitor of chariot wheels, spinning wheels, locomotive, car, truck, and airplane wheels, steering wheels, and the light, strong, tangentially spoked bicycle wheel.

"A major side-branch from the spoked wheel would bristle with the great family of rimless spoked wheels: water mill-wheels, windmills, fans, paddle wheels, propellers, food blenders.

"Returning our attention to the old solid wheel, we see that it branched into other unspoked wheels: the potter's wheel, the windlass, toothed gear-wheels, circular saws, rotating dials, phonograph turntables, movie projectors.

"As for the humble log roller that may or may not have been at the root of the wheel tree, from it emerged such differentiations as cane pressers, rolling pins, pulleys, rollers for forming sheet steel, rotary printing presses, hair curlers."

"That's very cute," said Kate, "with all its surprising anachronisms. But it's misleading. I'll grant that vehicular wheels preceded spinning wheels, but taken alone, vehicular wheels explain little about spinning wheels. Spinning implies fibers for making yarn and looms for using the yarn. Furthermore, your wheel lineages would make it seem that wainwrights developed gear wheels when it's much more likely that windmill carpenters did, or even makers of clockwork toys. And how could bicycle wheels have been made without wires and screws, and where are the trees of wire and screw lineages—"

"You're too quick for me, Kate," said Hiram. "Yes, the wheel tree is misleading for the same reason as biological family trees: Its imaginary diagram is based on linear thinking about development instead of web thinking. Development without co-development webs is as impossible for an economy as it is for biological development."

"The Icarus myth says it," said Armbruster. "The feathered wings his father made him were secured with wax, which melted when Icarus soared too near the sun. But feathers and wax are absurd generalities for differentiating human flight equipment. You've got me talking like you, Hiram."

"That's not what the myth meant to the Greeks," said Hortense. "After all, Icarus did fly, and Daedalus, his father, not only flew but landed safely. The Greeks weren't expounding technology. You've given the myth a hindsight gloss, Armbruster."

"The wreck of the *Titanic* makes essentially the same point Armbruster was making," said Kate. "At the time the ship was built and when it embarked on its maiden voyage in 1912, metallurgy hadn't advanced as much as engineering. Engineers had been able to design the largest man-made movable object, but the steel available to them couldn't withstand the stress of the vessel's size and it cracked under low impact with the iceberg. It was the best steel of its time."

"Icarus makes me shudder," said Hiram. "I'm nagged by thoughts of inventors ahead of their times. Sure, abalones demonstrate that it's practical to make first-rate ceramics at life-friendly temperatures, but that may be like ancient Greeks musing that birds prove flight is practical."

"Co-developments contrived for other purposes have to

be in place, eh?" said Armbruster. "A question for you, Hiram. Do old economic generalities eventually become obsolete in consequence of later development?"

"Possibly the very oldest economic generality is the practice of sharing," replied Hiram. "By that I don't mean random or inadvertent sharing but calculated, intended sharing as an institutionalized social practice. Along with us, our closest primate cousins, the chimpanzees and bonobos, go in for deliberate, socially formalized sharing. This suggests that the practice may go back to an ancestor common to the three of us, back to prehominid times. As far as economic life is concerned, the major differentiation that emerged from sharing was the practice of trading. A fossil form of English neatly records the developmental relationship. Old English had a verb meaning 'to give.' It also had a verb phrase meaning 'to trade,' which meant, literally, 'to give with worth'—that is, give for a price. Our word *sell* comes from a truncated portion of that phrase for trading, the part literally meaning 'give.'

"Time and again, human groups must have differentiated trading from both sharing and seizing. As a generality in its own right, trading has been a prolific source of further economic differentiations in transportation, communication, finance, markets, storage—"

"Also in development of legal codes involving contracts, ownership, and liabilities," said Hortense, "and social codes involving long-distance cooperation and relationships with strangers."

"Old as it is, sharing is still a potent generality," Hiram continued. "Economic developments still emerge from it. According to a report I ran across in 1996, a thriving cluster of commercial enterprises in Toronto ships old jeans to

Cuba, coats to Russia, and ripped cloth to India to be recycled into thread. What's left goes to Montreal, the report said, to be recycled into upholstery for automobile seats. This recycled clothing is given by people who are through with it. Sometimes they give it directly to the old-clothes sorters and shippers, and sometimes to charities, which sell it to the sorters. What's new about these commercial enterprises is the convenient service they worked out for donors and the labor-saving arrangements they worked out for themselves. They use phone calls or printed fliers to inform householders of the days when they can leave their donations in front of their dwellings. These arrangements have now been copied by charities that collect clothes."

"Notice that even those simple improvements use co-developments such as telephones, printing, and transportation," said Kate.

"Yes, and retail stores are drawn in," said Hiram. "Local secondhand stores, some of them run by charities and some not, get first pick of the donations. The old-clothes sorters who organized this efficient version of the ancient generality of sharing glimpsed possibilities for themselves in an economic niche that hadn't yet been adequately filled."

"Here's another instance of a potent old generality, although not nearly as old as sharing or trading," said Kate. "But it's so unexpected. Yesterday I edited a little item for our coming issue about a superior new type of computer chip. Its inventors—among other co-developments they used—adapted a technique for employing very fine copper wire, developed by Spanish jewelers in fifteenth-century Toledo. It got me thinking about obsolete generalities—how even the most obscure and frivolous are potentially economically fertile, provided that somebody who needs them can find them. Kinds of work are an economic equivalent of ecosystems' gene pools. So it would make sense to keep on the lookout for endangered species of work."

"Such as making buggy whips?" asked Hortense.

"Whips aren't an endangered species, and knowledge of how they're made is under no threat of extinction. Buggy whips are a tiresome cliché for obsolescence. However, manual typewriters are rapidly going extinct, and I doubt that mechanics are still learning to repair them, let alone make them."

"Anthropologists often record endangered techniques used by the people they study who live in remote places," said Hortense. "Then there are official patent-office records. And look how museum curators preserve specimens and sometimes information on ancient technologies for producing textiles, ceramics, glass, jewelry, and musical instruments. It seems to me we're pretty well provided with preservers of economic gene pools. But keeping track, as you suggest, Kate, is always bound to be important. A friend of mine who collects rugs tells me that some Turkish villagers are making beautiful Oriental rugs again, as fine as the finest antiques, thanks to reclaimed knowledge that was almost lost after aniline dyes replaced vegetable dyes around 1900. Besides making subtler and mellower color, vegetable dyes preserve the wool better. What's more, villagers who became idle dependents when harsh chemical dyes were being bought from outside now have work finding and preparing local plants. This affects the weavers' morale—I suppose they were resentful of people who didn't contribute while they themselves were hard at work—and the improved morale clearly affects the quality of the weaving, my knowledgeable friend claims."

"But, obviously, the skills of vegetable dyeing hadn't been lost from the gene pool of work," said Kate.

"Almost," said Hortense. "Saved barely in time. A few great-grandmothers still had the knowledge. Some information was hunted down in journals and diaries kept by nineteenth-century travelers."

"Notice the emphasis you've put on the old and beautiful," said Kate. "That's all to the good, but what about humdrum work and products going extinct right now? Some of them not all that old, either. Armbruster, this record you're making right now could possibly soon be lost irretrievably. Fifty reels of taped interviews made forty years ago became important to a Canadian investigative commission. Although the Viennese technology employed in making and playing back the tapes had once enjoyed an international success, an international search turned up not one machine to play back those tapes. Control of the speed with which the reels wound and unwound as their diameter changed—that was the problem. Recovering the content of the tapes was as daunting and delicate as restoring artifacts from ancient sites in caves and bogs. Computers have developed so rapidly that few are left which can decode information recorded only twelve years ago. The 'Knowledge Age' is going to become the Lost-Knowledge Age unless preserving specimens of work is taken as seriously as we've begun taking preservation of specimen varieties of apples and beans. Another thing," said Kate as an afterthought. "Knowledge of how to choose good transit routes seems to be going extinct, too, judging from cities that construct expensive transportation lines along ridiculous routes, then wonder why they're underused."

"That's because people who knew where—and why—to run a subway or streetcar are all dead or long retired," said Armbruster. "Traffic engineers try inappropriately to use what they've learned about truck and passenger-car routes. A different problem. But we're digressing. Hiram, I accept your point that our economies imitate the way nature develops. Let's move on."

Hiram frowned and looked dismayed. "I'm afraid I haven't been clear," he said. "Economic development isn't a matter of imitating nature. Rather, economic development is a matter of using the same universal principles that the rest of nature uses. The alternative isn't to develop some other way; some other way doesn't exist.

"Thousands of years before anyone had a glimmer of evolutionary or biological development processes, people were fostering differentiated strains of grains. Thousands of years before anybody was aware of symbionts such as mitochondria or chloroplasts, people were combining materials and devices that had radically different economic lineages. Even today, when educated people are aware of symbionts in the rest of nature, inventors who combine silicon chips with typewriter keyboards—or any other devices and materials with different economic lineages—aren't imitating animal cells and mitochondria. Rather, they're using universal principles of development and co-development for the good reason that no others are available. Economic development is a version of natural development."

"This is an intellectually interesting way to look at economic life," said Armbruster. "But what you've just said implies that it's academic information. People don't need to recognize the universal processes and principles to engage in using them. So is there any practical value or advantage in knowing that economic development is differentiations emerging from generalities?"

"Yes," replied Hiram. "It tells us that development isn't a collection of things but rather a process that yields things. Not knowing this, governments, their development and aid agencies, the World Bank, and much of the public put faith in a fallacious 'Thing Theory' of development. The Thing Theory supposes that development is the result of possessing things such as factories, dams, schools, tractors, whatever—often bunches of things subsumed under the category of infrastructure.

"However, if the development process is lacking in a town or other settlement, things either given or sold to it are merely products of the process somewhere else. They don't mysteriously carry the process along with them. To suppose that things, per se, are sufficient to produce development creates false expectations and futilities. Worse, it evades measures that might actually foster development."

"Such as?" asked Armbruster.

"Think about how the process works and therefore what it requires," said Hiram.

"Well, it requires economically creative people."

"Yes, and we human beings come by creativity naturally. Some people have more of it than others, whether by nature or nurture or both. Time and time again, it pops up in the most unexpected places.

"Now, suppose portions of a population are prevented from exercising economic creativity and initiative because of discrimination attached to gender, race, caste, religion, social class, ideology, or whatever. This means that the kinds of work those people do are automatically sterilized, so to speak—they can't be generalities from which new differentiations emerge. If categories of people doing specific kinds of work can't use those kinds of work as bases for development, it's unlikely anybody else in that economy will. The chip inventors Kate told you about can't see the same economic niches as the old-clothes sorters I told you about, and vice versa. It takes many kinds of work to develop and co-develop an economy."

Hortense spoke up eagerly. "This is why societies that are oppressive to women and contemptuous of their work are so backward economically. Half their populations, doing economically important kinds of work, such as cooking and food processing, cleaning and laundering, making garments, and concocting home remedies, are excluded from taking initiatives to develop all that work—and nobody else does it, either. No wonder macho societies typically have pitiful, weak economies."

"Serfdom, caste systems like India's, and slavery are more than a social outrage," said Hiram. "They're major economic handicaps, literally blocking development of the kinds of work that serfs, outcastes, or slaves do; and nobody else develops it within such a society, either.

"People don't need to be geniuses or even extraordinarily talented to develop their work. The requirements are initiative and resourcefulness—qualities abundant in the human race when they aren't discouraged or suppressed. That's clear from the changed behavior of many immigrants, or their children, when they move away from an oppressive traditional society to a more open one.

"In the Soviet Union, development initiatives and decisions were in the hands of bureaucrats. Just as you might expect, the development of bureaucratic and military work proliferated, but too little else was developed. The eight million employees in the bureaucracies that did the Soviet Union's economic planning were believers in the Thing Theory of development—but then, so are our own policy makers, politicians, and civil servants, for the most part.

"To put the usefulness of respecting the development process in positive rather than negative terms, we see why it's economically constructive to chip away at discrimination of all kinds. This is the sort of thing I mean by saying that bedrock economic processes not only impose limits on what we can do and how we can do it but also present invitations to work along with them."

"What about monopolies?" asked Hortense. "Wouldn't it be good development policy to avoid monopolies?"

"Yes, because by monopolizing various fields of work, they monopolize generalities of various kinds, the way postal systems, for instance, monopolized mail services until recently."

"But isn't there such a thing as natural monopoly?" protested Armbruster.

"The only one I can think of is the sun," said Hiram. "It holds a monopoly on the basic source of light, but the sun doesn't prevent us from kindling fires and switching on lightbulbs—"

Cutting Hiram short, Kate protested, "Organisms don't scruple to suppress competitors. Black walnut trees exude juglone, a herbicide that suppresses undergrowth. Knapweed devastates ranches. Besides poisoning livestock, it emits a herbicide that inhibits other plants. What about wolves and birds, when they stake claims to territories?"

"Juglone may be an adaptation to thwart parasites rather than to monopolize resources," Hiram replied. "At any rate, natural herbicides aren't very effective for establishing monopolies. Black walnuts don't dominate earth's forests today and never did, even before their wood was recognized as unusually valuable. As for wolves and blue jays, they're analogous to landowners who post their fields against hunters and warn that trespassers will be prosecuted. An economic monopoly controls a market or a commodity."

"As if hummingbirds prevented bees from taking nectar and distributing pollen in orchards," said Hortense, "and argued that the restriction was natural because nature had raised orchard blossoms aloft."

"Development depends heavily on testing adaptations against competition," said Hiram. "It's fair to say that nature abhors monopoly, Armbruster."

"I take your point that monopolies suppress opportunities for development," said Armbruster. "But I wonder if monopolies can be dismissed as simply as that. Black walnuts or knapweed—perhaps they wouldn't get a foothold, would be extinct by now, if they didn't have a herbicide advantage. What I'm really concerned about, of course, is economic monopolies. At the time they're instituted, monopolistic enterprises are often quick, bright, daring, and creative. There was a time when postal systems were quick and bright, and so were transit systems, believe it or not. Many an electric utility, streetcar line, telephone system, railroad, and subway line has gotten up and running because it had protection against competitors. What's more, here's an economic justification: It can be more efficient to capitalize a monopoly than to disperse and dissipate available capital among competitors, who are undercutting each other and some of whom are bound to fail."

"Whatever the justifications for monopolies to start with," said Hortense, "they all end up dumbed-down, elderly, and hard to get rid of. Why should the holder of a transit-route franchise—who probably got it through corruption in the first place . . . but, corrupt or not, why should that holder be sheltered indefinitely from free competition with respect to vehicles, fares, hiring policies, and services? Think of how much litigation, aggravation, and time it took before the monopoly grips of the electric and telephone companies could be broken. Worse, think about the struggles of conquered people to throw off monopolies on salt, matches, and everything else that their conquerors wanted to buy or sell."

"You mean like the Hudson's Bay Company and the Dutch East India Company?" asked Armbruster.

"Typical of imperial economies," said Hiram, "and definitely not good advertisements for development. Hortense has a point. But Armbruster has one, too. Patent protection, which is a grant of monopoly protecting the holder of rights to an invention from competitors using that invention, recognizes Armbruster's point that protection from competition can be useful to development of something new, but patents also recognize Hortense's point, as they grant protection for only a limited period.

"Standardizations are also stultifiers of development," Hiram went on. "I don't mean standardized goals, necessarily, but rather standardized means."

"Give us an example," said Armbruster.

"We want and need standards for results of sewage treatment," Hiram replied. "But it's folly to want standardized methods for reaching those results. To prescribe methods automatically blocks development of better methods. This principle, by the way, applies to all manner of activities. Windows don't demand standard frames. As my grandmother Jenny used to say, 'There are more ways to kill a cat than choking it to death on butter'—a folk saying that suffered a glitch in translation, no doubt."

"Surely growth is an important factor in economic development," said Armbruster. "But you haven't said anything about it. You haven't so much as mentioned the word. I've been listening for it."

Hiram looked tired. He ran his fingers through his thin hair, was silent for a moment, then said, "Development is qualitative change. Expansion is quantitative change. The two are closely linked, but they aren't the same thing. In some ways, economic expansion is more puzzling than development. Expansion baffled me until my father hit on an insight that had eluded me."

"I'd like to meet your father," said Armbruster. "Where does he live?"

"In New Jersey. Tell you what. Since expansion interests you, why don't you and Kate come over to my place in Hoboken for an afternoon and evening? Hortense will be there, too, and I'll invite my father. You can bring the recorder if you want. But I warn you, Armbruster, you'll have to endure information about expansion in ecosystems."

"When you think about it," said Kate as she was putting on her coat, "it's odd that we have to refer to the rest of nature to recognize what we ourselves have been doing with our economies."

" 'Know thyself,' " said Hortense. "Sounds like straightforward advice, but we can't do it by looking only inward. We learn about ourselves partly by learning about others and how we relate to them. Groups of people recognize group identity not merely by looking at their own groups but by comparing themselves to other groups and observing their relationships with them. Maybe human beings can't learn what it is to be human merely by looking at human life. Hey, I've constructed a fractal!"

Chapter 3

THE NATURE OF
EXPANSION

Hiram's house was an urban brownstone-and-brick from the turn of the century with a balustraded front stoop and tall windows, like its identical neighbors. The living room, where Hiram's father rose from a wing chair to greet Kate and Armbruster, was furnished haphazardly but gave a pleasant impression of uncluttered, unpretentious comfort. Built-in bookshelves, rather than pictures, dominated its walls. Behind it, Kate glimpsed a dining room with closed doors that, she later learned, led to the kitchen and to a bedroom wing jutting into a small back garden. Hiram's office was underneath, on the basement level.

Mr. Murray was not the pinstriped figure Armbruster and Kate had visualized. With his weathered face, flannel shirt, and L. L. Bean boots, he looked more the ecologist than his son. When Kate addressed him as Mr. Murray, he said, "Please call me Murray. Most people have since I was a boy, because of name conflations."

"Hiram says you like the numbers with the names," said Kate.

He beamed. "A tribute to the memories of my grandfather and father—both fine men who knew when to let go."

"Let go of what?" asked Armbruster.

"Let go of the destiny of the next generation. Interested?" Taking Armbruster's nod as permission, he went on, "My grandfather was a dairy farmer in upstate New York—very progressive. He had his own little dam and generator well before any public utility came into those parts. No milking machine, though—they hadn't been invented. He tried unsuccessfully to rig up a power beater for his butter. He used to send tubs of butter without ice off to expositions in Europe and once won first prize—in Belgium. He hung the certificate in the barn, joked that it encouraged the cows. He believed through and through in scientific farming and sent my father to the agricultural college at Cornell with the idea he'd take over the farm."

"And he didn't?" prompted Kate.

"No, civil engineering was the exciting thing for a young fellow then. My father switched to the engineering college. His first job was surveying for aqueducts supplying New York City with water from Westchester. Then he made a career in subway design. Worked up to assistant chief track engineer."

"What happened to the farm?" asked Hortense.

"Sold to a cousin in 1920. He lost it in the Depression. The next owner failed, too, and then came a family that lived in the house summers but didn't farm. The farm doesn't even exist now. In the seventies, it was cut up for roads and parking and a mall—looks like hell. The brook was put in a sewer pipe."

"What about you?" Armbruster asked.

"Enrolled in the engineering school and shifted to economics, with some courses in agriculture. I intended to specialize in agricultural economics, but after the war I found my feet as an analyst in a new mutual-funds outfit and there I stayed. An interesting job, trying to keep one or two jumps ahead of surprises. My wife, Amber, had an entirely different background; it's why Hiram has this house. Amber's father, Joel, was a classic penniless immigrant. He came over in 1908, a young fellow from a village near Kraków. He learned cobbling from his father."

"He bought this large house as a shoemaker?" asked Armbruster.

"Oh no, he started out polishing and cobbling in a shoe repair shop in the Wall Street district. The shop owner was from Poland, too. The city used to be full of little shoe-repair shops, one every few blocks. You can hardly find one nowadays. People throw out their old shoes, and a lot aren't even made of leather or designed to be repaired anyhow."

Kate, harking back to her thought that skills are an economy's equivalent of gene pools, asked, "Is cobbling in danger of going extinct?"

Murray looked surprised at the question, squinted in thought, then replied, "Oh no, not as long as enough people buy custom-made shoes for themselves. After three or four years, the shop owner lost his health and sold Joel the shop on credit. Then Joel did two things: He sent back to the village for Jenny, his childhood sweetheart, and he started stocking up on shoe findings: heels, sole leather, laces, eyelets, polish, thread, needles, thread wax—that kind of thing. He put in a telephone and hired a delivery boy and sold findings to other repair shops in lower Manhattan. Jenny kept the books and—"

"Did she know English?" asked Hortense.

"She picked it up fast, but she always did have a heavy accent. The findings business grew, and Joel gave up cobbling. They took a little office in what's now become fashionable SoHo, which was then a warren of small manufacturers. Jenny looked around her and persuaded Joel to add findings for belt and handbag makers: clasps, buckles, frames, specialty braids, lining materials, and so on. Jenny followed the fashion papers and on Sundays looked at the Fifth Avenue church crowds. Nothing about shoes, belts, and handbags escaped her. She and Joel employed four salesmen at their peak. Amber took the commercial course in high school and graduated top of her class. Smart as they come—that's where Hiram gets his brains."

"How did you meet Amber?" Hortense asked.

"Soon after the war. She was visiting a secretary friend in the fund office where I worked, to watch a parade on Broadway. I gave her a basket of ticker tape to throw out the window, and we took to each other. Amber and I never lived in this house. She rented it out until Hiram grew up, then let him have it and left it to him when she died. This street ran down, but Hoboken's come up—I told Hiram it would when artists and singers began to move in."

"Both my tenants are musicians," said Hiram. "One's doing so well I'm afraid I'll lose her. She plays tenor sax in a little band. They started out in clubs here in Jersey, then Manhattan, and now she's on tour most of the time. When I fixed up the apartments, I thought one would be for Joel, my son, but he took off for the West Coast."

"What does he do?"

"Hard to say. Right now he thinks he wants to be a social worker and lobbyist, helping homeless people. We'll see."

"He may be back here yet," said Murray. "There's plenty of homelessness right here in New York. You might say it isn't a declining activity like shoe repair."

"Let's get down to business," said Hiram. "Where do you want to set your recorder?"

"You said the subject was to be economic expansion," said Armbruster, plugging in his machine and testing it. "Start talking."

"Let's begin with natural expansion. The most amazing demonstration of expansion is the sheer volume and weight of biomass on the earth. It expanded from nothing before life began and now includes the huge conglomeration of earth's plants and animals, among them, of course, billions of human beings. Earth's biomass is even larger than we commonly notice. Microorganisms are thought to account for as much as seventy-five or eighty percent of total biomass volume, maybe more. Microbiologists now think that more microorganisms live deep underground than at or near the surface. Bacteria even live underneath glacial ice. Added to all the living things are stored remains: fossil fuels; compost and worm droppings in the topsoil; ancient seashells composing chalk, limestone, travertine, and marble; wooden beams of buildings; paper; the clothes you're wearing and trillions upon trillions of other relics of lives lived."

"There couldn't have been that expansion and diversity without development and co-development," said Kate.

"Right. Development and expansion are tightly interlocked. They make each other possible. But the puzzle is how. Theoretically, each successful new thing might crowd out an equivalent volume of old things, yet that doesn't happen—not in economic life or in the rest of nature. Why not? Let's think about how biomass expands. We may see it happening if we look in the right places at the right times."

"We used to see it expanding on the old farm when we

passed by on our way to the Adirondacks," said Murray. "We saw it changing after the cows were sold off and the place was going to ruin."

"Whether ruin or recovery depends on your point of view," said Hiram. "As an ecosystem, it's ruined now by parking lots, paved roads, and buildings, but for a while those abandoned pastures and hayfields zoomed into luxuriant life. You can see the same phenomenon in abandoned cornfields, say, or barren tobacco fields, where the bare dirt doesn't even have a cropped grass cover at first. But left to itself, an abandoned field is invaded by vagrant seeds that produce a spotty crop of weeds, at first hardly enough per acre to make a decent covering for the bottom of a wheelbarrow. Gradually, hardy burdock and thistles are joined by more delicate chickweed, dandelions, tufts of wild grass, vines, bramble shrubs, pioneer saplings, lichens, and moss until every inch of soil is tenanted. Yet strangely enough, expansion of the biomass continues—and even more rapidly than when there seemed to be more room for expansion. Saplings grow taller, then are crowded out by still taller species. Patches of violets thicken; undergrowth tangles more tightly. The scant animal life of worms, beetles, ants, and butterflies is joined by other insect species, along with birds, little mammals, and who knows how many more varieties of bacteria multiplying in leaf mold, animal droppings, and corpses. A few bobcats or a pair of foxes sneak in and join mice, shrews, voles, skunks, rabbits, snakes, woodpeckers, and owls."

"Now you're exaggerating," said Murray. "I doubt that any bobcats took up quarters on the old farm. Foxes, yes, and maybe some orphan house cats. And once, poking around when passing, I glimpsed a raccoon. But it wasn't wild enough—or probably large enough—for bobcats, Hiram."

"Okay, scratch the bobcats. Anyhow, at some point the Noah's Ark part of the restoration is complete. All the current species in the vicinity who will find the environment congenial have come aboard. Yet the biomass still expands. Trees get larger, moss thicker, vines longer, seeds more abundant, mushrooms bulgier, earthworms fatter, squirrels more abounding, lichens lumpier. What are they expanding on? The rich environment? But the ensemble itself made the environment rich by expanding. How can this be?"

"You're leaving out the sun," said Kate.

"Yes, the sun comes into it. Very much so. A so-called self-sustaining system is not really *self*-sustaining, of course. It needs infusions of energy from outside itself. That's true of every system on the planet, including weather, river, and ocean systems. We ourselves need fuel. Machines need fuel or some other kind of propelling energy, like horse- or manpower. The energy sources of some kinds of microorganisms seem to be infusions of heat and chemicals from the interior of the earth, but with that exception, the ultimate source of earth's energy infusions is sunlight. In an ecosystem, chloroplasts living symbiotically in plant cells capture raw sunlight, and from that point on, the energy infusions which organisms receive are conversions of the sun's energy.

"But energy infusions are only the first half of the energy story. The second half is energy discharge. Eventually, a system discharges all the energy it receives. Energy/matter can be converted from various forms to various other forms, but it can neither be created nor destroyed. To be sure, it can be stored for short or long periods, as in corpses before they decay, timber, books, buildings, fossil fuel, even limestone. Ultimately, a system's discharged energy is lost to it by radiating outward. That's why all living systems need either continued or sporadic infusions of new energy.

"So an ecosystem can be thought of as a conduit through which energy passes, with many or few transformations of energy/matter during its trip through the conduit. The interesting question is what happens in the conduit.

"In some ecosystems, not much happens. Sunlight falling on a desert barren of life heats sands and rocks, but when night falls, even that quantity of temporarily retained energy radiates outward. In this case, the passage of energy is swift, simple, and vanishing, leaving no evidence of the passage. It must have been like this when sunlight fell on earth's primordial rocks and empty seas before life began. Deserts aren't as bereft of life as they may seem, but because they lack water—or, near the poles, because of cold—only a pittance of a desert's received energy is stored in tissues or discharged in metabolic, neural, and muscular activities. The same can be said also of sunlight falling on warm and well-watered—but paved-over—land or poisonously polluted lakes.

"Contrast that with energy flow through a well-developed forest ecosystem. In the forest, energy flow is anything but swift and simple, because of the diverse and roundabout ways that the system's web of teeming, interdependent organisms uses energy. Once sunlight is captured in the conduit, it's not only converted but repeatedly reconverted, combined and recombined, cycled and recycled, as energy/matter is passed around from organism to organism. Energy flow through an intricate conduit of this kind is dilatory and digressive. It leaves behind, in complex webs of life, ample evidence of its passage.

"No other terrestrial ecosystems can compete with tropical rain forests in sheer variety of species. At first thought, it seems as if the tropics' warmth throughout the year and the blazing power of tropical sunlight must be responsible for the abundance. However, when a tropical forest is cleared, the soil bakes and hardens. Rainfall also turns destructive, leaching minerals out of soil no longer interlaced with roots and protected by forest canopy. For those reasons, crop yields are typically mediocre, dwindling so rapidly that after a few years the land is hardly worth planting. Merely in themselves, sun and rain, and even atmosphere and soil, don't account for either biomass expansion or biomass variety."

"What's the mysterious answer then?" asked Armbruster.

"It isn't really mysterious. The answer is the forest's multiple uses of energy received within its conduit before the energy is finally discharged from the system. Multiple energy use requires diverse, interdependent users. The principle can be stated like this: *Expansion depends on capturing and using transient energy. The more different means a system possesses for recapturing, using, and passing around energy before its discharge from the system, the larger are the cumulative consequences of the energy it receives.*

"Now, before you say it, Armbruster, I will: Does this have anything to tell us about economic expansion? If so, what? And if not, what other principle or process expands economies?"

"I used to think I knew the answer to that," said Hortense, with the object of giving Hiram a respite from his monologue. "I thought of my answer as the picnic principle. The more people the picnic must feed, the more people there are to carry the picnic baskets. People to carry and people to feed correspond nicely. If the picnic principle worked economically, idleness and neediness couldn't exist together at the same time."

Hiram, who had poured himself a glass of water and wiped his brow, laughed. "You're always surprising me, Hortense. Creating an economic equivalent of the picnic principle has been a preoccupation of modern governments and their advisers. The most straightforward attempts to deal with simultaneous idleness, need, and undone work have been make-work projects, or subsidies to maintain economically unsuccessful enterprises. More subtle attempts rely on various investment incentives, transfer payments, work-sharing schemes, and economic protectionism, on the one hand, or free trade, on the other hand.

"But prescriptions based on the picnic principle don't work. Some that seem workable in the short run become ineffective or even lead to disasters, such as double- and triple-digit inflation, in the longer run. Sometimes full-employment policies pursued no matter what result in declining productivity and shortages, as happened in the Soviet Union—a situation expressed in the sardonic joke whose punch line is: 'We pretend to work and they pretend to pay us.'

"Whether fiddled with or left alone, some economies obdurately refuse to expand to meet either their people's needs or their people's potential as workers. Others expand with so much sporadic vigor that guest workers or immigrants are invited to the picnic to help carry and share the sandwiches. London booms, while much of northern England languishes in long-term depression. Almost every country of any size suffers persistent regional inequalities.

"In sum, the exasperating fact that idleness and need co-exist is all too obvious. But remedies are anything but obvious. If you're on the watch for mystery, Armbruster, cast your eyes on economic expansion."

From the depths of his chair, Murray spoke up: "Hiram told me about biomass expansion, the same as he's explained it to you. Then he asked me how settlements—towns, cities, or any settlements—expand their economies. I told him that the root cause of expansion was competitively successful export work, which I'd been taught and still believed at the time."

"Do you mean foreign exports?" asked Kate.

"Any exports, foreign or domestic. Any kind, too. Common sense tells us that if a town's truck factory expands its workforce to five thousand jobs from a previous three thousand, the town will enjoy expanded sales of clothing and groceries; more schoolteachers are needed, and another half dozen doctors. Maybe rents and house prices rise, stimulating residential construction. Food, clothing, shelter, education, health—the basics. More people to feed, more workers to pay for the food. Your picnic principle at work, Hortense. You can think of other additions to the town economy that are less vital and the jobs they generate, too; maybe a video-rental addition to the sporting-goods store, even a body-piercing and tattoo parlor. A printer gets out more copies of the union local's newsletter, and so on. No need to labor this point further.

"Common sense and observation also tell us that if a settlement loses net export jobs, other sales and jobs in the place dwindle. Subtract all export jobs from a settlement—that can happen to a town or village when a mine shuts down, a fishery fails, or a factory closes—and probably all other jobs in the place disappear too: ghost town.

"So, logically enough, economists call local jobs 'multiplier' jobs, distinguishing them from jobs devoted directly to export work."

"When you say 'devoted directly to export work,' does that include people working in firms that supply things to exporting enterprises?" asked Hortense. "Like a local paint-manufacturing company that sells to the truck plant?"

"No," Murray replied. "Exporters' suppliers fall into the multiplier category, indirectly supported by purchasers of exports, same as the grocery stores. Of course, the paint plant may export part of its output, in which case some proportion of its work is in the multiplier, and some not. Most cities have large numbers of small exporters, and small ones are more likely to draw on local accountants, lawyers, maybe designers, repair people, and so on than large exporters, who draw more on their own personnel. So it's logical that cities have higher multiplier ratios than towns and much higher than villages. In a good-size city, local and exporting work overlap a lot, because any one accountant or designer, say, may do work for customers in the local population and for other local businesses and may find some customers at a distance, too.

"But however simple or complicated the multiplier response to export growth may be, the conventional idea has been that export work drives or leads a settlement's economic expansion. And a total national economy is quantitatively the sum of net expansion or shrinkage in its whole sum of settlements. If we want to carry that still further, the global economy is quantitatively the sum of net expansion or shrinkage in the whole sum of countries. Which is why so much economic hope rests in free trade: more trade, more exporting; more exporting, more multiplier jobs."

"I suppose this doesn't satisfy you, Hiram," said Armbruster. "For you, it's probably too far removed from the convoluted ways that biomass expands. But it satisfies me. It's straightforward. It accords with common sense and observation. So what's the problem?"

"That's what I thought, too," said Murray. "I took it for granted, for decades. But export-multiplier ratios are not as neat and tidy as I've made them sound. When they're looked at critically, the ratios can be puzzling. Hiram asked me questions about them for which I couldn't find satisfactory answers. Ratios vary more widely than one would suppose if there's such a direct cause-and-effect relationship. They also vary significantly from time to time in the same place, without clear reasons. Still worse, ratios can contradict the theory itself. For instance, in Los Angeles at a time when export work declined precipitously, other jobs didn't decline in response. They increased stupendously, faster than jobs were increasing in any other settlement in America at the time. This was in the 1940s, starting near the end of the war. The anomaly can't be dismissed as some weird California thing. Back in Shakespeare's time, for instance, London's economy was behaving just as irrationally. On the other hand, Detroit's ratio decreased while its automotive export work boomed.

"Every contradiction can be rationalized as a special case. So can all the other anomalies. But a process that is thought to be systematic and ordained, almost like the cause-and-effect workings of a machine, but obviously isn't all that mechanistic, is a process that invites intellectual suspicion.

"Let's face it, I said to myself," Murray continued. "This export-led idea of expansion is actually only a hypothesis, even if it's sufficiently entrenched to be considered a theory. Maybe it's wrong, or else so partial a truth that it's as misleading as it is illuminating. I stopped dismissing Hiram's biomass information as irrelevant. This was economic heresy! I kept an open mind while I turned ecosystems and biomasses around in my head, even if I couldn't grasp their application to the economies of settlements."

Hiram now cut in: "Then one night, late, he called up and sang out, 'I've got it! I really think I've got it.' You tell them, Pop."

"The thought came to me," said Murray, "that we were looking at the wrong end of settlements' energy conduits. What are exports? End products of a settlement's economy, that's what. They're discharges of economic energy. To be sure, they become imports in some other place, but at the location where they've been produced, they escape from a settlement's energy/matter economic conduit. A discharge."

Armbruster attempted to speak, but Murray waved him to silence. "I know it sounds outrageous, Armbruster, but hold it until I finish. Discharged energy doesn't—and can't—also suffice as driving energy. If it could, the result would be a perpetual-motion contrivance." Armbruster began furiously scribbling on a notepad, snorting occasionally, but Murray ignored him and plowed on. "At that point in my thinking, I looked up perpetual motion in the encyclopedia. Sure enough, inventors and backers of perpetual-motion devices attempted to force their equipment's discharged energy to double back and drive the next turn of the wheel, or the next change of water level in a container, or whatever other motion was required to keep the thing in operation. The schemes were ingenious and they sounded as plausible as the dickens. Think of the fuel that could be saved if they worked! But none of them worked. Willy-nilly, they discharged energy in their operations, and the discharges that escaped as discharges were unavailable as power for driving the contraptions."

"Even a prize Jersey cow can't survive by merely drinking her own milk," said Kate. "That's fundamental. It's an iron law of nature that every organism and every machine needs infusions of new energy from outside itself or it comes to a halt."

"If exports are a settlement's economic discharges, then what are its received infusions of economic energy?" Murray asked rhetorically. "Imports! Besieging armies and blockading navies have always known that. So obvious, but until I began thinking about settlements' economies as instances of natural energy-flow I couldn't see that imports came in at the receiving end of their conduits, exports left at the discharge end, and the interesting question was what went on within the conduits."

"False analogies!" sputtered Armbruster, unable to contain his scorn. "An ecosystem gets its sunlight free, for nothing. But a settlement has to earn its imports with export work. So it's absurd for you to construe exports as something lost to settlements' economies! They aren't lost, because payments for exports buy imports. I don't care how prize Jersey cows survive or what the laws of thermodynamics say. Exports are clearly the driving force, because they buy imports and support multiplier jobs to boot. Payments from customers come to more than the cost of materials going into exports and upkeep of the labor producing them. Payments, Murray! And before money, people bartered goods for exports. There's your infusion of economic energy from outside—payments!" He glanced at his pad. "Oh, and here's the clincher. According to your logic-chopping about energy flow and discharged exports, settlements would have to start their economic lives with imports—before they worked up a way to earn them! Absurd! How could they do that?"

"You're right about that last point," said Murray. "It's the first major question that our energy-flow hypothesis had to address. I myself was at a loss to answer the question you just posed, Armbruster. How might one account for imports first and exports only subsequently? Hiram supplied the answer. You explain, Hiram, how a settlement obtains imports before it earns them with exports."

"I want an answer that goes deeper than a claim that settlements can get imports for start-up on credit or charity," said Armbruster. "Economic life predates foreign-aid programs, investments of multinational corporations, and political pork barrels. Those are relatively recent froth on economic life. Besides, they fail as often as they succeed. They're probably even a drain on economies."

Hiram, finally getting in a word, said, "Seeds and embryos get started in life with free, unearned energy/matter contained in eggs, gifts that start their development, gifts from—"

"Of course!" Kate interrupted. "The egg's stock of initial starter energy! I should have thought of that myself. A settlement's initial imports are as unearned as sunlight, Armbruster. They arrive across time instead of across space."

"What on earth are you talking about?" asked Armbruster.

"Natural resources," said Hiram with a grin. "Every settlement starts with at least one useful resource, maybe several, already in place as a gift from nature. It's an inheritance from earth's past development and expansion. If a resource or a combination of resources weren't there already, neither would a settlement be there.

"A starter resource can be fertile soil," he went on. "Or it can be any number of other things: wild animals, flints, nut trees, clay, ore, a waterfall, fossil fuel, hot springs, a beach. At the very least, a settlement starts with a site, a fine resource if it's a protected, convenient place for people to meet and exchange goods and services. Venice's initial significant resource was sea salt, which Venetians traded to Constantinople. The salt wasn't earned by export work. It was a gift from the sea, and it earned other imports. The quaint old stock-exchange building in Copenhagen carries a motif, in wrought iron, of herring curled into the fetal position of human embryos, symbolizing that the herring trade was the embryo of the city's economy. The burghers of Copenhagen understood how their economy started—with a gift from the sea—and they wanted posterity to remember that fact. Think which came first in embryonic Copenhagen—the unearned presence of herring in adjacent waters or Copenhagen's exports of herring. Rome's most significant initial economic gift was pasturage for cattle, which provided Romans not only with meat but also with leather for exporting to older and richer Etruscan settlements to the north. Those Etruscan cities exploited nature's gifts of iron ore, both for their own use and to export iron to older and richer cities in the Middle East. Osaka, Chicago, Paris, and San Francisco are random examples of many, many settlements whose chief—or sometimes only—initial economic asset was being a good site for a trading hub."

Hiram paused and looked at Armbruster to invite a possible protest, but although Armbruster was still frowning, he had simmered down and was silent. Murray spoke up instead: "Initial resources for settlements' economies aren't earned by export work, but all the same they're earned in a different way—earned by combining gift resources with human effort. The Venetians concentrated salt by cleverly directing seawater into series of evaporation ponds in their lagoons, probably at first to get salt for their own use, then subsequently for export, too. Fishermen in the North and Baltic seas toiled and risked their lives for herring—again, probably at first for themselves and their families, then for export. Early Romans had to exert themselves at herding, slaughtering, and skinning cattle and properly tanning hides. Mines and quarries make heavy work. To satisfy merchants at a trading hub, people located there must provide inns, porters, goods containers, warehouses, security, travel supplies, and transportation.

"This leads into the interesting question of what goes on in the conduit," Murray went on. "Beginning with the very start of a settlement and continuing for as long as the place maintains an economy, human effort is combined with imports. Also combined with imports is equipment—some of it imported and some not. And the most important ingredient qualitatively—although not always quantitatively—is human capital. That means skills, information, and experience—cultivated human potentialities—resulting from investments made by the public, by parents, by employers, and by individuals themselves.

"In the conduit, human labor and human capital transform imports—take them apart, recombine them, pass them around, recycle them, and by all these means stretch imports received into the conduit."

"You keep introducing bizarre new expressions," complained Armbruster. "How do imports get stretched?"

"You already know, Armbruster; you know so well that you take it for granted," Hiram interposed. "Here's an example: A painter uses canvas and pigments, a sculptor uses stone or metal, and possibly all those materials are imported into a settlement where the artists are at work. But materials account for only a small portion of the worth of a work of art; the value of the materials has been stretched within the conduit. The value added by the artists isn't a multiplier of export work, yet there it is. Works of art are extreme and vivid examples of import stretching, but other kinds of producers also stretch imports."

"Old Joel and Jenny stretched imports," said Murray. "So did their customers, who used findings to repair shoes and make handbags and belts."

"No disrespect to Joel and Jenny intended," said Hortense, "but they didn't produce anything. One could argue that they soaked up part of the wealth created by producers. Otherwise we have to grant they were making something from nothing, which is as impossible as perpetual motion."

"Joel and Jenny were producing services," said Hiram. "You can't call their work of searching, sampling, assembling, and distributing 'nothing.' They were adding human capital to other matter/energy in the city conduit. What Joel, Jenny, and their salesmen added was sufficiently concrete and useful to purchasers of findings to be worth part of the cost of the items.

"All services add human labor and often, as well, yield from investments in human capital, to whatever imports happen to be used in the service work. Additions of human capital that fast-food servers contribute are small compared with the amounts of imported food and Styrofoam they handle. On the other hand, most design work uses large proportions of human capital compared to imports, as do almost all sorts of research, experimental, and development work, whether institutionalized or informal. A newly developed item may go into export, but until it does, it's not an export; nor is it necessarily a multiplier of existing exports.

"Many imports, even after they're initially transformed or otherwise stretched, are then passed around some more, fragmented, recombined, recycled, and stretched further."

"How do you mean, fragmented and recombined?" asked Hortense.

"Here's a rather simple instance," said Murray. "A building is a composite of imported materials, locally transformed materials, and engineering and other design services. It has ten tenants, say: a dental laboratory; a maker of eye-catching signs . . ." He ticked them off on his fingers as he spoke: ". . . a cake and pastry baker, for its own two retail shops and for restaurants; a dance rehearsal hall—"

"The thumps of the dancers are going to make the cakes fall," said Kate.

"No they aren't," said Murray. "This loft building was constructed in 1910 to support heavy stamping presses. The thumps of dancers are nothing. This isn't some throwaway Barbie-doll suburban mall. The rehearsal hall . . . then, let's see, a photo-developing, copying, and poster-framing service; a place that sells florists' supplies and does floral arrangements that are too ambitious for ordinary shops; it teams up with the cake bakers to produce splendiferous effects. A tea blender and packager; a team of cabinetmakers specializing in display fixtures but game to tackling almost any carpentry or furnishing problem short of war work—they won't touch war work; a bank branch down on the ground floor next to a major importer of Oriental rugs.

"Each of these tenants uses fragments of the building and its utilities, hence fragments of the imported materials it contains. Each tenant combines those fragments with its own pieces of equipment and flows of materials, some of which are imported, some partially imported. Combinations change as tenants turn over.

"This building owner, I've heard, has plans for an eventual complete overhaul of plumbing, wiring, elevators, and interior finishes, to convert the place into fashionable loft apartments." Murray glanced at Armbruster, who was silent, so Murray continued. "A metropolitan economy teems with thousands of enterprises, most of them supplying goods or services, or both, to one another or to the local population, or to both. Such an economy can't be accounted for quantitatively as a response only, or even primarily, to expanding exports."

Hiram, after a glance at Murray, took up the argument. "But such an economy can be accounted for quantitatively as a result of dilatory and digressive uses of imports that have entered the conduit—exactly as biomass expansion in the forest can be accounted for as a result of dilatory and digressive uses of energy from the sun that have entered the conduit. Listen to this carefully: In an ecosystem, the essential contributions made within the conduit are created by diverse biological activities. In the teeming economy, the essential contributions made within the conduit are created by diverse economic activities. In both systems, thanks to the diversity with which received energy is used, fragmented, and reused, that energy/matter leaves much evidence of its passage through the conduit. Do you see now why I say that the interesting question is what goes on in the conduit? And now we can see why and how an ensemble grows rich on an environment that the ensemble itself made rich."

"An ensemble making itself rich by its own existence—it sounds like a trick," said Murray. "But it's really no more tricky than the old adage 'Waste not, want not.' In this case, 'Recycle, reuse, recombine, employ symbiosis.' I've come to the conclusion that economists would do better to abandon export-multiplier ratios and turn their attention to import-stretching ratios."

"How would you get such a figure?" asked Armbruster, finally entering the conversation again.

"In principle, nothing could be simpler," said Murray, "except that the necessary statistics aren't collected. Combing them out wouldn't be all that easy."

"The most truthful information that statistics give us is that for some reason researchers have become interested in what they're counting," commented Armbruster.

"Only two figures would be needed," said Murray. "First, the value of imported goods and services a settlement receives, no matter what they are and how they're to be used and, second, the value of the settlement's total production of goods and services during the same period of time—say, three years. Dividing the second figure by the first would yield a ratio of total economic activity to imports. Of course, import figures would include the value of local natural resources, such as oil or standing timber, used during the period.

"At best, the ratio would be crude," Murray went on, "because it would understate total economic activity by leaving out volunteer and unpaid do-it-yourself activities, which are appreciable and valuable; and of course it would leave out black- and gray-market activities, which don't get into records. But done sequentially, in three-year or five-year blocks of data, such ratios would focus attention on what's happening in a settlement's conduit; they would tell whether activity in the conduit is increasing or decreasing relative to imports received, including local natural resources that are processed. Ratios would also register the presence or absence of economic self-refueling, which we haven't discussed yet. Essentially, such a ratio would track the trend of value being added within a settlement—but not as an absolute quantity; rather, as a ratio to energy being received. It would show whether a settlement's conduit is behaving like the conduit of a lush ecosystem or a semi-barren one and, in either case, which way it's heading."

"By a semi-barren conduit, do you mean one in which most of the energy received bounces right back out?" asked Hortense. "Like a desert ecosystem?"

"Exactly," said Hiram. "Settlements can answer to that description if most of their imports whiz into export work and go right out. For instance, in an American or Canadian rural settlement that concentrates on cash crops, imports can be enormous in proportion to the numbers of workers producing the crops. There is plenty of energy being received from outside; plenty of variety too: expensive farm machines and their repair parts and fuel, trucks, seeds, fertilizer, fencing, maybe irrigation equipment, pesticides, weed killers, construction components for storage bins and barns, and of course consumer goods. Almost all of the imports are incorporated directly into the work of tilling, planting, tending, harvesting, storing, and transporting the crops to be exported and into feeding, clothing, and sheltering the farmers and their families. Therefore, the passage of almost all the settlement's imports through its conduit is economically direct and simple—straight through from one end to the other.

"Naturally, imports used like this leave behind only a pittance of other economic activity as evidence of their passage: a few routine retail establishments and entertainment or other gathering places, along with basic public services—which may require subsidies from tax yields of more diverse economies. And naturally, most young people who don't inherit a farm or aren't attracted to farming have to hunt for work somewhere else.

"Simple settlements—meaning settlements with simple, direct energy conduits—don't always depend on natural resources, such as farmland, ores, or timber, although they often do. Some depend on single-service operations such as isolated military bases, prisons, or large resorts. Others are company towns that depend on a single large industrial enterprise, such as a textile mill, a pulp mill, an oil or aluminum refinery, a hydroelectric plant, or an automobile-assembly plant. Don't mistake what I'm saying. I'm not saying the exports of simple settlements lack value—they're often very valuable as imports into other settlements. But as imports into other settlements, they're received energy, and how valuable they are as received energy depends upon the conduits of the settlements they enter. When they go into settlements that are good at stretching imports, they carry with them a potential of being economic expanders. If they merely go to other simple settlements, whether domestic, foreign, or both, they lack that potential."

"This energy-flow hypothesis of economic expansion explains why countries whose settlements are overwhelmingly rural are invariably poor, no matter how small or how large their exports and imports may be," said Murray. "It also explains why the richest—which means the most expanded—economies are diverse economies. The practical link between economic development and economic expansion is economic diversity. Here's the principle, which applies to both ecosystems and the economies of settlements: *Diverse ensembles expand in a rich environment, which is created by the diverse use and reuse of received energy.*"

"The limited nature of resources and the law of diminishing returns—dismal facts that made economics the dismal science," said Armbruster. "Now you throw in import stretching, resource substitutions, and human capital, a resource which yields increasing returns—not diminishing returns—the more it's used, and economics seems to be the hopeful science.

"You've beaten me down on settlements' initial gift imports. But even a chick, after it's out of the shell, has to scratch for itself. It still remains that subsequent imports must be paid for by exports. That still leaves exports as the driving and expanding force of economies, even if it makes hash of your energy-flow economics."

"We can go into your objection tonight," said Hiram. "Let's eat dinner first. I suggest we walk over to the Clam Bar."

At dinner, while Hortense, Hiram, and Kate were comparing their impressions of a Japanese movie, Armbruster asked Murray how he occupied himself.

"Twice a week I tutor high school students who need extra help in bookkeeping; that's volunteer work, investment in human capital—although it's not formally recognized as such. Wednesday nights I give elementary accounting lessons to adults. For that I advertise in a couple of community weeklies and charge tuition. That's self-investment in human capital on the part of my students. I also keep bees—at present, three hives."

"Isn't that arduous?" asked Armbruster. It struck him suddenly that Murray looked frail in his rugged flannel and boots.

"The hardest part was getting a legal exemption. The town zoning says you can't keep chickens, cows, goats, or bees. Horses, dogs, and cats, on the other hand, are socially acceptable. I rounded up people to support me, went in for publicity, hounded officials, made it a local issue, and finally wrestled out a bee variance."

"On economic grounds?"

"Oh no. I did emphasize possible benefits for gardens and ornamental trees. But what really swung support and won the day was when I told them about the educational benefits for children: field trips right in town for elementary-school classes in science and environment. Parents and teachers care a lot, you know, about adding more substance to kids' education—public investment in human capital. I get plenty of visitors."

Chapter 4

THE NATURE OF

SELF-REFUELING

"We've refueled ourselves," said Hiram as the five friends settled themselves comfortably in his living room after dinner. "But if we think we're now at leisure, we're mistaken. For our own purposes, each of us is busily converting clams, salad, bread, wine, and strawberries into energy. We'll each use part of this energy to acquire more food for ourselves, other meals. I'm drawing your attention to one of the two main characteristics of self-refueling systems. Part of the energy each takes in from outside itself is spent to capture subsequent infusions of energy, and part of that to capture more infusions, and so on, repeatedly."

"Obvious," said Armbruster. "How else could an animal—or for that matter a plant—keep going?"

"Oh, some have found other means," said Hiram. "In symbiotic partnerships, one partner often supplies fuel to the other. Seeds, eggs, and infants of some species inherit captured energy before their own refueling equipment kicks in; as we discussed this afternoon, human settlements inherit natural resources before they earn imports.

"Machines depend on outside agents to push a treadle, turn a crank, set a sail, hitch a horse, fill a woodbox or tank, plug into a power line, change a battery. Machines lack equipment for refueling themselves, their symbiotic value to us consisting of other activities we've chosen for them. On the other hand, weather systems, which are also inanimate, do drive themselves with energy they capture from the sun."

"What about wind-powered machines that use part of their energy to shift their vanes into the wind in response to shifts in direction of the wind?" asked Hortense. "I'd call that self-refueling. My telephone battery recharges itself while the phone's in its holder. I grant you, the recharger conks out if it isn't plugged into the electric line—but then, I don't dig my own clams and pick my own strawberries, either."

"You're so good at finding blurry lines, Hortense," said Hiram.

"That's the way lawyers think," said Armbruster. "It's how they earn their living—afford to buy more food for themselves."

"Windmills do come close to being self-refuelers," said Hiram. He paused and scratched his ear. "But even the most efficient don't capture fuel supplements they require, such as oil for their bearings, let alone spend some of their energy to keep their refueling equipment in repair, as healthy organisms do.

"The other main characteristic of self-refuelers is that they possess equipment appropriate to the fuel they use. Suitable equipment is so important that its breakdown is as fatal to an organism as the disappearance of its fuel. Appropriate equipment is the 'self' of self-refueling. Cows are equipped to feed on grass, but we aren't. Termites get along on wood, but cows can't. Appropriate equipment often includes symbiotic bacteria, as well as suitable food-capturing and -digesting equipment. Because of the necessary matches between equipment and fuel, self-refueling systems are finicky. Each system has its own integrity as a discrete, tangible unit. One organism's waste is another organism's dinner. Self-refueling has no generalized form—only many, many specific forms."

"But what about the Gaia Theory," asked Hortense, "the idea that earth and its atmosphere, rocks, water, and living matter constitute an integrated, live organism?"

"Each of earth's ecosystems contains numerous species of self-refueling microorganisms, animals, and plants, each of which has its ways and means of refueling. The ecosystems of the earth and their denizens are linked by the common atmosphere and lithosphere, which they share and which have been jointly shaped and formed and changed by the actions of life processes. But shared links don't erase the tangible specificity of discrete self-refueling organisms, Hortense. You can't blur those into one abstract life."

"Is *self-maintaining* merely an alternate way of saying *self-refueling?*" Hortense persisted. "What about *self-relying, self-sustaining,* and *sustainable?*"

Armbruster glanced around the room for a dictionary. "I already looked them up, Armbruster," said Hiram. "Those expressions overlap with *self-refueling,* although we tend to give them moral overtones. For example, *self-reliance* is generally taken to be so admirable that lack of it is seen as unfortunate or even bad. *Sustainable* commonly applies to the practice of drawing on renewable resources at a rate no speedier or greedier than the rate at which the resources can renew themselves; the practice implies environmental morality. Self-refueling is a basic natural process. As Kate pointed out, no matter how efficient a cow may be, if it doesn't self-refuel, it's a dead cow. Self-refueling is so fundamental to survival, and to all the other processes of life made possible by survival, that conceptions of whether it's a good or bad thing are pointless. Even units that are not self-refueling, such as machines or viruses, depend on self-refueling helpers at one remove or more."

"I suppose you're slowly leading us up to an economic principle," said Armbruster. "Let me guess. You're going to tell us economies are self-refueling. That's what I've been trying to tell you myself. Payments earned by export work earn imports. So the payments are an economy's fuel!"

"I'm going to give you a different picture of economic self-refueling," said Hiram. "Although my analysis embraces yours, it digs deeper by addressing the question of where exports come from. As you mentioned, even a chick, once out of the egg, must scratch for itself. I agree that exports earn imports. But what if the export work is lost? For instance, if the company moves away from a company town or fails, the place is left without export work and its payments. It may be rescued, perhaps, if it's given another exporting enterprise by another company or perhaps by a government. In that case, the settlement is behaving like a machine: Somebody has to refill its tank for it, and if nobody does, the machine stands still. Not all settlements are self-refueling. But some settlements do self-refuel. They fill their own tanks by generating their own export work."

"Hmmm," Armbruster murmured. "Are you saying that some settlements serve as incubators of new export work for themselves?"

"Very well put," said Hiram. "Remember I mentioned my tenant the sax player? She used to play her imported French saxophone in local clubs—those were the incubators in this case—but now she brings back export earnings from tours. Besides that—here comes a co-development web—her band's recordings, which are made across the East River, in a studio in Queens, now enjoy more export sales than they rack up in this metropolitan area."

"It's not uncommon," said Murray, "for designers, accountants, and other professionals to get a foothold in a local economy and then find distant customers as well."

"Interesting and worthy," said Armbruster, "but rather trivial considering the size of this city's economy and its needs for imports."

"In the aggregate, slides from the local economy into export work aren't trivial," said Murray. "Furniture; jewelry; nursery-school equipment; scrap compactors; architects' services; importing and distributing services; insurers', lenders', and other financial services; medical services; ethnic, health, gourmet, or other food preparations; house-renovation items—almost anything that makes it in a metropolitan market finds at least some customers outside that market, often a great many. Furthermore, even taken singly, exports arising out of work in the local economy aren't necessarily trivial. In my old job of analyzing corporations' prospects, I used to dig into their histories. These outfits were all publicly traded firms, some among them big conglomerates with histories of mergers. Many had national and some had international markets. Those last included corporations that had originated abroad. Every firm—and every subsidiary—had gotten a tangible, localized start somewhere.

"Those tapes you're using in your recorder, Armbruster—I noticed they're made by 3M, a Minneapolis company that started out with a handful of employees trying to make sandpaper. It got its capital from a local supplier of goods to plumbers. The sandpaper was inferior, but while attempting to improve it, the company made some unusual glue, excellent for housepainters' masking tape. The tape enjoyed a fine local and export success."

"This isn't masking tape in my recorder," said Armbruster.

"No, but with one thing leading to another—new differentiations emerging from prior generalities and new combinations of them with co-developments—the company produced whole families of tapes, among them, in due course, your sound-recording magnetic tapes."

"But many successful exporting enterprises never went after local customers first," said Hortense. "Not all exports incubate that way. Armbruster's book publishing company began exporting books from its start."

Armbruster nodded.

"Then why did you establish your company here in New York?" asked Hiram. "Hortense tells me you love Nantucket Island. Why didn't you start it there? Or maybe on an idyllic Caribbean island?"

Armbruster laughed. "Everybody who falls in love with Nantucket fantasizes earning a living there. I did too. But unfortunately it wasn't practical—too inconvenient for my purposes. A good thing, I suppose, or Nantucket would be like Manhattan instead of being Nantucket."

"In other words," Hiram pressed him, "you needed networks of this and that—convenient co-developments."

"Yes. Another reason I chose New York was that I'd served my editing and publishing apprenticeship here, so I knew the ropes in New York."

"All American computers nowadays are actually manufactured abroad," said Murray, "mostly in Taiwan. Only two decades ago, Taiwan's major exports were cheap toys and garments. But the production networks and skills built up there in the course of producing toys and garments, and especially in manufacturing machinery for producers of toys and garments, made Taiwan's economy and people versatile enough that new export work could be generated there when sales of their former big exports dwindled."

"But garments and cheap toys still enjoy big export markets," said Hortense. "Why would those made in Taiwan dwindle?"

"Taiwanese labor used to be very cheap," said Murray. "But the economy lost that advantage to its own prosperity, which brought higher wages. Settlements lose older exports for many reasons: competition from elsewhere, obsolescence, poor management, relocations, import replacements in former customer cities—"

"I have an objection to what you two have been telling us," Hortense interrupted. "You sound as if there are only two types of settlements: big cities containing great economic diversity, on the one hand, and small, machinelike, economically monotonous settlements, on the other. That doesn't check with the world I see."

"You also sound as if there are only two types of ecosystems," said Kate. "That doesn't check with reality, either. Natural ecosystems display every gradation between lush and semi-barren."

"Valid criticisms," said Hiram. "Murray and I have been dwelling on extremes because they clarify the processes we're discussing. But of course you're right; in fact, many gradations exist in the very same cities over the course of time. Even the greatest cities, ancient or modern, started off small and simple—even semi-barren or close to it."

"A cousin of my grandfather's immigrated to San Francisco in 1849, when he was a young fellow just out of his teens," said Murray. "He planned to become a prospector and join the gold rush. Came by ship like almost everybody else. The city was a bunch of tents and a few shanties on the beach. Pretty much all there was to its economy were rough-and-ready suppliers to prospectors and each other—men selling whiskey, flour, bacon, pickaxes, pans, and mules; prostitutes were already there, too. Drovers were bringing in steers, hunters were bringing in game, and cooks were throwing together stews, frying fish and pancakes, and baking sourdough biscuits. The day after my grandfather's cousin arrived, while he was still getting his bearings, he bought a pet monkey from a sailor. The next day, he sold it to another sailor. Then he bought a turtle from a prospector and sold it to a bartender. He never did take off to the gold fields. He kept buying and selling animals. Next, he started breeding pets; I forgot to mention he was a farm boy back home in Pennsylvania. The pet company he founded flourished for more than a century on fashionable Maiden Lane in downtown San Francisco. During the first half of the twentieth century, it also supplied African, Asian, and South American animals to zoos and circuses in many parts of the country."

"I can't describe anything that exotic," said Hortense, "but I happen to know two farm women who started their businesses by selling goat cheese, and jam made from local berries and orchard fruits, to the restaurant of a rural resort near their homes. When they did that, they were strictly suppliers to an exporter, weren't they? The jam maker put up attractive packages of her assorted jams and preserves for resort guests to buy and take home with them, and the cheese maker copied her. They became exporters on their own account, right? Both buy labels from a local kid with a computer printer. He does their brochures, too, because now they also export by mail order. Who knows, maybe when he's older he'll export some service or product. Popping up in New England and on the West Coast are movements trying to take pressure off people's demands for more logging work or other resource-exploiting jobs by encouraging value-added work benign to rural and wild ecosystems. It's a rural form of import stretching—by adding higher proportions of human labor and human capital to timber and other natural resources. Remember, you said given natural resources should be thought of as imports, so if they're stretched, that figures as import stretching, too. Some of my friends think cities are obsolete now because modern communications make it easy to link into webs of customers and suppliers no matter how small the settlement you're in."

"Book publishers spring up in the unlikeliest little places nowadays," said Armbruster.

"Before you jump to the conclusion that cities are obsolete," said Hiram, "you should be aware of a version of self-refueling that converts towns into small cities and small cities into large ones. We human beings are terrific copycats. It's one of our main traits, and on the whole we're good at it, when we see something we like."

"You mean, I go to a party, say, and taste guacamole dip for the first time?" said Hortense. "I get the recipe from my hostess and make it myself for the next party I give?"

"Monkey see, monkey do," said Kate.

"Yes, and the second time you made it, as I remember, you experimented a bit, added a touch of mace," said Hiram. "Fractals again. This same pattern of behavior occurs on many different scales. People find both small and large economic niches behaving essentially this way. For instance, a woman living in a village may notice that her neighbors pick up croissants and other goods at a bakery-café when they go to the nearest town on errands. She does this, too. So she takes a chance and opens a bakery-café right in the village. Her imitation is a local replacement of a retail service and some goods that villagers have been importing. By being a copycat she's created a couple of new village jobs. But in a village, opportunities to make a living by copying imports are very limited for two reasons: As markets, villages are small; and in any case, a village doesn't include a wide enough range of skills, experience, and equipment to produce a wide range of the various kinds of goods and services it imports. Being small, it's just not that versatile economically.

"Let's move to a larger scale, to a settlement considerably more versatile because it's been steadily building up its varieties of export work and suppliers to its export work. In the process of earning imports, Armbruster, it has simultaneously been diversifying its capabilities at producing and has also been enlarging its local markets for imports. At some point, such a diversifying and expanding economy does acquire the ability to replace significant ranges of its imports—in fact, chains of them.

"Young San Francisco reached such a point about twenty-five years after the gold rush and a subsequent period of wild lawlessness. Its little enterprises then buckled down to producing an array of goods and services for shippers and for successful and unsuccessful silver mines and miners in the hinterland. Wages and profits bought, among other things, conveniences and amenities that were nearly all imported from eastern cities. Among these imports were jams and preserves, stocked by a grocer named Cutting, who came from Boston, and ordered them from a Boston wholesaler. By the way, commercially bottled and canned fruits were a Paris innovation; copycats in England shipped them across the Atlantic, and then copycats in two American cities, New York and Boston, took to making and exporting those products—that's how they reached San Francisco.

"It occurred to Cutting, who may or may not have been aware of the history of the products, that he could improve his niche in the San Francisco economy by producing his own jams and preserves for the same customers he'd already been supplying with the imports he was planning to imitate. This wasn't as simple as it sounds, because he had to persuade farmers on the outskirts of town to devote wheat and cattle land to peach, pear, cherry, plum, and apricot trees. Starting in that small way, it was the beginning of California's ultimately huge commercial fruit and vegetable production, but that stupendous rural economic expansion was still in the future.

"At the time Cutting started making jam, he automatically shifted his purchases of imports. He bought more imported sugar than previously, and he also imported empty glass jars. His profits, as they materialized, went into purchases that included imports, which of course didn't all go into the jars of jam. His venture was so successful that other local people imitated it. Some varied his recipe—went in for producing canned beans and peas previously imported from the East Coast. Together, preservers and canners composed a large enough market for imported containers that somebody found it profitable to make glass jars right there in San Francisco, while other entrepreneurs imported sheets of tinplate to make cans."

"Let me guess," said Armbruster. "Eventually somebody put up a rolling mill and began importing pig iron and ingots of tin in place of imported tinplate. But you must have skipped something, Hiram. I don't understand how the local market for jams, preserves, and canned goods grew large enough to justify a local glass factory and a rolling mill."

"It wouldn't have grown large enough," said Hiram, "except for the fact that the chain of import replacements that started with the jam was only one among scores of other replacements that occurred simultaneously or in rapid succession. Smiths were replacing imported tools; carpenters and artisans were imitating imported household and business furnishings; seamstresses were imitating imported gowns; and so on. In the aggregate, the resulting jobs directly and indirectly enlarged markets for all import replacers. Together, these enterprises radically altered the composition of the settlement's imports, and kept altering them as shifts of imported purchases led to further replacements. And as swift sequels, many of San Francisco's import replacements became exports from the city. By the 1930s, canned vegetables and canned and dried fruits were the city's second-largest industry; tin cans and other tinware were its fifth-largest.

"We hardly recognize a settlement to have become a little city," Hiram went on, "until it has experienced an abrupt burst of unusually rapid growth, during which it has filled itself out with at least all the goods and services that are commonly produced locally in little cities of its time and place but which the settlement earlier imported. All great cities—now we're looking at this process on a big scale—have experienced repeated bursts of import replacing and shifting. These bursts, when they occur in large cities, are mighty economic forces. Remember the anomalies of Los Angeles and Shakespeare's London, both of which flourished mysteriously while their exports happened to be temporarily in serious decline?"

Murray spoke up. "Replacements of imports are imitative but not always slavishly imitative. They commonly incorporate economically advantageous improvisations in materials, or in methods of production, and sometimes changes in design. If imitations improve items, replacements are especially apt to become successful exports."

"Such as?" asked Armbruster.

"Japanese sewing machines, to mention one example of thousands. Sewing machines first reached Japanese cities as imports from America, where they'd been invented. In Japan, although they were expensive, they were popular. Locally made replacements, starting in Tokyo, cost less than imports because of improvised, economical production methods. Instead of being produced in expensive, integrated factories like the imports, the replacements were produced as bits and pieces in many small, already-existing machine shops and were assembled by contractors; the production paid for itself as it grew, rather than requiring risky, large initial outlays. Next, these machines became exports from Tokyo to other Japanese cities—many of which also replaced them with local production, adding their own improvements and changes adapted to local uses of the machines. This is how Japan eventually generated some eight hundred sewing-machine companies and became the world's preeminent producer, especially of machines for doing various specialized types of industrial stitching. Japanese cameras, radios, cars, and business suits are replaced imports but, except for the suits, not slavish imitations."

"I'm surprised that such a modern process occurred—as you mentioned this afternoon—in Shakespeare's London," said Hortense.

"Import replacing extends back into time immemorial,"

said Hiram. "Archaeologists call it economic borrowing, and prehistorians call it dissemination—or, less accurately, diffusion—of techniques. Armbruster, I want you to pay close attention to what I say next. This is a process that enables cities to capture new imports *without drawing upon payments for exports*—a feat you believed is impossible. Look at it this way: When a settlement's economy shifts to purchasing new imports as an automatic consequence of replacements, that economy has everything it formerly had plus the new imports to which it has shifted. Some shifted imports go into replacement work; others are pure extras—additional energy received into the conduit from outside as surely as if they'd been bought with payments for export work. But they're acquired by means that bypass necessity for added export payments."

Armbruster, Hortense, and Kate all started to speak at once. Kate prevailed, with this objection: "I don't think import replacement happens in the rest of nature, Hiram."

"This form of self-refueling is peculiar to economies, but it works only because it employs principles common to all self-refueling," Hiram replied. "Perhaps you've forgotten those two basic principles. First, a portion of received energy must be devoted to capturing further energy. That's exactly what an import-replacing city's economy does. By replacing some of its previously received imports with its own production, it uses them to capture other imports. Second, it must have appropriate equipment, suited to the acts of capturing and making use of its fuel. The relevant equipment in this case is the settlement's current ability to produce. That requirement is why chains of replacements typically start with goods and services that are easiest to replace at a specific time and in a specific place and replacements can proceed to more complex and difficult ones as a settlement's production capability—its refueling equipment—diversifies and expands. Cutting didn't try to make his own jars. That step awaited both a larger local market for jars and an entrepreneur who understood glass manufacturing. What were you going to say, Hortense?"

"From what you say, cities have a means of getting imports without having to earn them. It seems like an unfair advantage over other places."

"It's an economic advantage, no doubt about that," said Hiram. "But the process creates cities, which is why it is cities that have this advantage. As for self-refueling being a way of acquiring imports without earning them—now you're using Armbruster's limited definition of *earning,* as if the word has to mean 'getting payments for exports.' Replacing imports requires effort, skills, capital, and courage, just as generating exports does. Replacements are a different way of acquiring imports, not a means of getting them free, for nothing, without exertion and risk. What did you want to say, Armbruster?"

"Earlier, you mentioned Detroit as an anomaly because the proportion of its local jobs shriveled while its export work boomed," said Armbruster. "Just the opposite of Los Angeles and Shakespeare's London. Why was that?"

"Detroit became specialized at the expense of diversity," said Murray when Hiram gestured to him to answer Armbruster's question. "Detroit's economy had actually been excellent at generating exports and replacing wide ranges and many chains of imports until its most successful export work—automobile manufacturing—came to dominate the city's economy. By the mid-1920s, the city's versatility had gone into reverse. Independent local suppliers to the car industry dwindled because the car manufacturers absorbed many of them into their own companies and stopped buying from many others in favor of filling their own needs for supplies internally. Surviving independent suppliers concentrated on shaving prices for a few huge customers, didn't seek other customers, and didn't develop nonautomotive sidelines. For another thing, skilled workers didn't break away from the booming automobile industry to found other kinds of enterprises, seek other economic niches. I myself admired Detroit's specialization, industrial integration, and efficiency. It's only by hindsight that I recognize it was a prelude to economic stagnation."

Hortense, sounding cranky, said, "Why am I only now hearing about import replacing and shifting? Why wasn't I taught about it in college? It goes on openly, after all."

"You still wouldn't be taught about it in college," said Murray. "When Hiram first talked to me about self-refueling and import replacing, I tried to disabuse him of the notion that he was onto something basic and important. My generation of economists placed strong faith in economies of scale; I thought of decentralized production—local production—as old-fashioned, a vestige of economic life that hadn't learned modern, efficient organization. I assumed that he was interested in a local form of protectionism that could only penalize consumers, a nostalgic view of economic life. These were standard economic views.

"Hiram drew my attention to the fact that companies often establish branch plants or branch offices in cities to which they've previously only been exporting goods or services but in which their markets have grown large enough to justify production at the market. He pointed out that companies do this forced by nothing except their own economic self-interest. 'Why do they do such a thing?' he asked me. Thinking about it, I had to acknowledge that economies of location often override and outdo economies of scale.

"Another reason I was skeptical was that I remembered a short-lived fiasco of the 1970s that went by the name of 'import substitution.' Poor countries were provided with loans and expertise to construct factories intended to produce various things they imported—electric motors, shoes, lightbulbs, medicines, whatever. At the same time, they could save on foreign expenditures."

"Well, that sounds sensible enough," said Armbruster. "Isn't it the same as import replacing?"

"Only in the abstract," said Murray. "Remember, self-refueling isn't an abstraction. It's specific to discrete units with tangible equipment suited to the purpose. The import-substitution programs fixed upon items selected abstractly, from statistics on imports. Factories were located in semi-rural economic deserts because jobs were most needed there. Although labor costs were low, the factories and their imported equipment and imported managers and supervisors were expensive. Markets weren't at hand; co-developments were missing; nothing meshed. When the intended substitutes for imports could actually be produced with reasonable speed and reliability—an expectation seldom realized—the products cost more than equivalent imports. Intended customers couldn't afford them. That's why the import-substitution fad was short-lived, but even so it bankrupted Uruguay and almost bankrupted a number of other countries. You can see why import substitution got a bad name."

"It deserved the bad name," said Hiram. "A volatile process responsive to specific conditions in specific places was ignorantly straitjacketed."

"Technocrats will never understand what you're saying," said Armbruster. "For the rest of us, I suppose the lesson is something you said early on. Natural processes put limits on what we can do and how we can do it." He glanced at his notepad. "Here's what I get from your disquisition this evening, Hiram: Settlements have two ways of using part of their imports to capture further and different imports. They can incorporate some imports into new exporting enterprises, whose payments earn imports. They can also replace some imports with local production and shift purchases to other imports. Both self-refueling methods are open-ended, and each abets the other."

"Well summarized," said Hiram. "I'd only add that, for obvious reasons, enterprises in import-shifting cities are wonderful customers for goods and services—shifted imports—that can't be produced locally there, at least not yet; these typically include innovative goods and services created in other settlements. Of course, that especially interests me. Innovative, environmentally benign methods of producing energy, food, and building materials, goods that are recycled, recyclable, and biodegradable, goods that eliminate toxic ingredients—all these require not only creators but customers. Historically, the earliest solvent customers for innovations have been enterprises and individuals in prospering, import-shifting cities.

"So far," he continued, "we've discussed three master processes that govern successful economic life as surely as they govern the rest of nature: development and co-development through differentiations and their combinations; expansion through diverse, multiple uses of energy; and self-maintenance through self-refueling. In the interests of convenient exposition, I've taken these up one at a time, but they interlock."

"Nature abhors monotony," said Kate. "Diverse ecosystems are so much more stable than one-crop plantations. Diversity itself protects ecosystems against total devastation by diseases and abnormal weather that demolish one-crop plantations."

"Maintaining economic stability is dicey," said Hiram, "because what's required is dynamic stability. If you're game, we can go into that subject in one more session." He paused inquiringly, and when each of the four nodded agreement, he went on. "We can have only one more session—" and here he raised his hand in a victory sign "—because I'm happy to report that one of my clients is ready to get into pilot production! And another may be on the verge. I'll have to be at their beck and call to help with a million details; also, frantic emergencies are sure to crop up. So I suggest we meet here next Saturday in the morning. The weather's turned warm enough for a picnic lunch in the back garden. We can eat and talk at the same time and maybe wind up before dinner. If not, we'll still have the leeway of evening."

"Good," said Kate. "I like the sound of 'leeway,' because I've been thinking about an idea to try on the rest of you if there's time."

"I'll leave the recorder here," said Armbruster, "presuming it has an invitation to spend the week."

Chapter 5

EVADING COLLAPSE

Except for Murray, who had spent the night in Hoboken and been up since dawn, it was a listless group that assembled Saturday morning. Kate grumbled at the prospect of sitting indoors on a beautiful day. Armbruster was uncharacteristically clumsy with his recorder. Hortense stared apathetically into space, and Hiram, sipping his second cup of coffee, sounded bored and prepared to bore others as he droned, "Fundamentally, self-correction consists of—"

"I thought the subject was to be dynamic stability," protested Armbruster. "I looked it up."

"The essence of dynamic stability is constant self-correction," said Hiram. "What's your definition, Armbruster?"

"*Dynamic* is from Greek for 'power' or 'strength'; it carries a sense of motion. *Stability* is from a Latin root meaning 'to stand,' and when it's coupled with *dynamic*, it carries a connotation of resisting overthrow or collapse."

"Energetic steadiness," said Murray.

"Excellent," said Hiram, his customary eagerness returning as he gulped the last of his coffee and set down his cup.

"Before you go any further," said Armbruster, "just what kinds of dynamic entities are you referring to?"

"Every kind of system that is neither inert nor disintegrated. This includes all living systems: ecosystems, organisms, cells composing organisms, microorganisms. It also includes many inanimate systems: rivers, the atmosphere, the crust of the earth. Human settlements, business enterprises, economies, governments, nations, civilizations—they're all dynamically stable systems. Stability implies its opposite, instability. All dynamic systems are in danger of succumbing to instability, which is why they need constant self-correction. If and when a dynamic system decisively loses stability, it either collapses into inertia or disintegrates. Then eventually maybe something else dynamically stable engulfs it, or something new organizes itself from the pieces."

"Much the same as saying all things alive are in peril of death," put in Murray.

"Death always wins in the end," muttered Hortense gloomily.

"No dynamically stable system lasts forever," said Hiram. "But the wonder is that such vulnerable systems endure at all, succeed each other, and even flourish for their time under the sun. Dynamic systems have resources and methods for evading collapse. Of course luck plays a part, but even when luck favors them, dynamic systems must continually correct themselves with timeliness and accuracy. Resources and methods for doing this fall into four categories, of which—"

"Only four!" exclaimed Kate. "I'd have supposed dozens

for economies alone; and in the rest of nature—what? Millions? Trillions?"

"Actually, four are quite a lot," replied Hiram as he distractedly searched his jacket pockets for imaginary cigarettes, then checked himself. "Nature is prodigal with details but parsimonious with principles. I'll sketch out the categories in this order: bifurcations; positive-feedback loops; negative-feedback controls; and emergency adaptations.

"To anticipate myself, let me warn you that seldom does each individual mode of correction stand alone. Weblike, each affects the other modes. Dynamic systems can and do use all four modes simultaneously. Let me also forewarn you that none of the methods of correction is perfect. Each conceals traps and can have treacherous side effects, which may be why dynamic systems don't last forever. But in spite of shortcomings, the modes of correction serve incomparably better than lack of corrections. In any case, they're what we have to work with and depend on, gratefully and warily."

"How do you know these four are the only means that dynamic systems have of correcting themselves?" asked Kate.

"I don't know that they are. They're the only ones I know of, either in economies or the rest of nature. It's possible, of course, that my interest in economies has influenced what I see in the rest of nature. All I can tell you is that these four are my best shot, and if you dig up others, more power to you.

"We're already familiar with the fact of bifurcations, because bifurcations are developments. But not all developments are bifurcations."

"Would you define *bifurcations*, then?" asked Hortense, who had begun to perk up.

"The word means 'fork,' like a fork in the road. It's a term chaos theorists use. Mathematicians call the same kinds of events discontinuities. Here's the correction principle: A system's instabilities of some sort can have become so serious that for it to continue operating as it has been is not a practical option. It must make a radical change—take a fork in the road, travel into new territory.

"Evolutionary history is stuffed with bifurcations. A momentous example from our own point of view was the emergence of air-breathing vertebrates from an ancestry of marine vertebrates."

"What instability did that overcome?" asked Hortense.

"Not known for sure. Lungfish had both gills and a primitive lung, suggesting that their habitat was swampland. The earliest to take to dry land may have inhabited swamps subject to severe droughts, or perhaps they were escaping fearsomely jawed predators who couldn't follow them onto dry land. Notice, I've assumed a localized start—necessarily so because bifurcations in species don't begin statistically; they begin anecdotally with individual adaptations. Successful adaptations spread because their possessors spread.

"An earlier example is emergence of multicelled organisms, which employ symbiotic divisions of labor not only within cells but also among cells—as we do. A plausible hypothesis has it that a rich and nourishing environment became crowded with stacked-up cells, some of which had no direct access to the environmental riches because of their interior positions in the stacks. Which cells took to specializing in which of the various tasks of life—probably at first as temporary episodes in their life cycles—would have been determined by their locations in the mass, as happens in simple multicelled organisms today and also in embryos of our own species as they develop. Location dictates their future. The hypothesis is plausible because unstable critical masses frequently spawn developments that don't occur in more spacious environments."

"Does that apply to economies?" asked Armbruster.

"Very much so," said Hiram. "The Romans built aqueducts when local springs, wells, and the Tiber became inadequate for the population. The subways built by modern cities when surface streets can no longer accommodate traffic, tall buildings serviced by elevators, and public-health and sanitation measures to forestall epidemics in densely populated places are other obvious examples.

"At some time prior to nine thousand years ago, some innovative hunting people took to saving captured game animals for breeding. That became a correction to uncertainties and instabilities of the hunting life. The oldest settlement with domesticated meat animals that has thus far been found, Çatal Hüyük in Turkey, already had a complex economy for its time, including sophisticated crafts such as weaving and copper working, along with much evidence of trade and a dense population numbering in the thousands. Hunting remained an important activity, alongside animal domestication. By hindsight, we realize how important animal herding was within the settlement's conglomeration of numerous other activities. To depend for meat on wild game was not to continue as a viable option for human beings once they became numerous and skillful enough to wipe out wildlife in their hinterlands, then either starve or interminably pull up stakes."

"A vegetarian diet could have been an alternative," said Hortense.

"Same principle. If anything, agriculture was a more momentous and more stabilizing new fork in the road, particularly as grain cultivation became combined with horticulture, arboriculture, animal husbandry, crop rotation, and appropriate tools, together making long-sustained farming possible.

"Bifurcations have complex consequences. They not only embody radically new practices; they change the very systems that give them birth or that adopt them by imitation. Accumulations of bifurcations alter the character of civilizations. We acknowledge this when we refer to the Bronze or Iron ages, to the Industrial Revolution or the Scientific Age. We try to anticipate historians of the future by calling our own times Postindustrial or Postmodern or the Knowledge Age.

"The rule that effective bifurcations change a system operates on the small scale, too. Fractals again. An individual business enterprise at risk of failing because its product is obsolete or because competitors are outdoing it may evade collapse by embarking on a new product line. But if it does, it must inevitably alter its own character—say, by wooing customers in whom it formerly had no interest, or by using suppliers it formerly did not need and perhaps influencing them to change as well, or by recruiting workers with skills and ideas different from those it formerly sought, or by changing its location, or by entering into joint ventures or mergers with other enterprises, or by any number and combination of changes. If its corrections to itself don't suffice, it collapses."

"In an ecosystem, a failed organism becomes food for more successful organisms or for newly arising life," said Kate.

Murray suddenly reentered the conversation. "That's just what happens in an economy. The failure's assets are sold off to purchasers who hope to put them to more succesful use than the failed enterprise did. Many a new enterprise gets its initial equipment at distress prices from bankrupt firms."

"The fact that successful bifurcations are timely poses more questions than one might suppose," said Hiram. "Bifurcations are corrective only before a system has collapsed. Later is too late. It follows that they must already be available—ready and waiting somewhere—before instability has become desperate or terminal. How does that happen?

"When Joel and Jenny devised a small-scale new departure for their little enterprise, they were not correcting an instability, which is why I've just called what they did a new departure, not a bifurcation. They could have continued as is, cobbling. But they responded to opportunity—in this case, the chance for a more promising economic niche. My biomimics are pushed by alarm about environmental destruction, but they're simultaneously pulled by opportunities to satisfy their curiosity and indulge their creativity—which, in their case, are powerful incentives. The pull of opportunity, including entrepreneurs' hopes of prospering, is the reason bifurcations can be ready and waiting before their invention or discovery comes too late to rescue imperiled systems. They frequently begin as sidelines to other activities—as herding was at first necessarily a sideline to hunting, or else where would the first domestic animals have come from? Sidelines are bifurcation incubators. Opportunity, not necessity, is the mother of invention. The necessity is seen by hindsight."

"Here's something that infuriates me!" Hortense burst out. "Misanthropic ecologists love pointing out that plagues and famines used to limit unbridled human population growth, with the implication that only such disasters or others they can think up will save the planet from unbridled and unsustainable multiplication of the human race. Those misanthropes aren't observant enough to notice that in prospering economies—where women as well as men are educated and where mothers can reasonably assume that their offspring are secure against plagues and famines and will become educated too—in those economies, women themselves voluntarily limit the number of their children. They do this even when religious authorities or the state forbid them to do it. They don't need plagues and famines—quite the contrary. Hiram, would you call birth control a bifurcation?"

"Yes. Those misanthropes who infuriate you, Hortense, have lost faith, if they ever had it, in the ability of the human race to rescue itself from collapse as a species. Birth control, like other bifurcations, began where it could feasibly emerge and has since been working its way further—in this case, wherever economic and social conditions for women and children are favorable for it. Voluntary birth control, when it's looked at in the distant future by hindsight, might even be ranked with agriculture and herding as a major stabilizing bifurcation.

"But give those misanthropes credit, Hortense, for grasping a very important point. While bifurcations may be fine at correcting instabilities, they also generate new instabilities. Ways of overcoming plagues and famines—to the extent we've done so—were bifurcations that generated such new instabilities as unprecedentedly rapid and prolific population growth and unprecedented worldwide stress on resources. We can be sure that forced birth control commanded by the state, as in China, will generate new instabilities there that can now only dimly be guessed at. Even more gradual and humane voluntary birth control injects new instabilities into social and economic life. For starters, it disturbs pension arrangements, immigration policy, and education.

"This is the trap hidden in bifurcations: unintended and unforeseeable consequences. Automobiles and trucks disposed of draft animals in cities, where their excrement, urine, flies, and din had become intolerable, along with the ever-mounting pressure they put upon farmland to supply feed. That was a fine bifurcation, but automobiles created new instabilities, which urgently demand correction in their turn. The trap of unintended consequences isn't owing to human shortsightedness or stupidity. It's inevitable in the nature of things. Earth's crust itself never finishes with correcting its instabilities, precisely because each earthquake, volcanic eruption, and adjustment of tectonic plates can be only temporarily corrective. The corrections themselves lead to new stresses and strains. Similarly, each evolutionary development, no matter how temporarily stabilizing it may be for some creatures, leads to destabilizations among others—"

"You can say that again!" said Kate. "Think of the new instabilities that afflict other creatures because nature cast us up!"

"We live on an eternally restless planet," said Hiram. "Its very creativity and fecundity require endless further corrections. No help for that. Pessimistically, we can despair at being trapped in economic and social systems impossible to perfect or even to make tolerably secure except, at best, for the time being. Or optimistically, we can take zest in the fact that the world affords, among its riches, endless streams of interesting and constructive opportunities to correct and correct and correct what we do.

"And remember, dynamic systems possess means in addition to bifurcations for holding instability and collapse at bay. Let's go on to the next category, positive-feedback loops.

"Here's a pleasing example of this category—a positive loop in a California coastal redwood forest. Mature redwoods require enormous amounts of water, about twice as much, on average, as rainfall delivers to their habitats. Yet redwood forests are so stable that—"

"*Were* so stable until we began cutting them at rates that, even now, threaten extinction," said Kate indignantly.

"Yes, but let me continue with my point. A coastal redwood lives to an age of about two thousand years; quite a demonstration of successful survival. Here's how their seemingly inadequate supply situation is overcome. With their fine and luxuriant needles, the trees intercept fog and strip its moisture; in effect, they take water straight from clouds. During a dry but foggy night, each tall redwood douses the ground beneath it with as much water as if there had been a drenching rainstorm.

"This beneficent process works as a loop. The growth of the trees is fed in good part from fog. Taller growth gives trees access to higher—hence additional—fog. Additional fog feeds still taller growth. And so on. Because of the height-fog loop, the trees themselves participate in keeping their environment stable. This loop was first scientifically measured by ecologists in redwood stands, but the height-fog loop has since been identified in various forests composed of pines and other tree species.

"We're already familiar with beneficent loops in economies, although I didn't call them that. For instance, exporters in a settlement support suppliers there; some suppliers become exporters on their own account; these support more and different suppliers; some of these become exporters; and so on. That loop intersects with a beneficent import-export loop: A settlement generates exports by combining some of its imports or resources with human labor and capital; this earns the settlement more and different imports; it uses some of these to generate further exports; and so on. That loop is one form of economic self-refueling. The other self-refueling loop is the powerful import-replacing and import-shifting loop."

"Ecosystems are crammed with loops," said Kate. "Plants support animals that help fertilize plants; luxuriant plant growth supports more animals; and so on. Salmon fry are nourished in streams of their birth habitats; nourishment makes them strong enough to swim downstream to the sea; in the sea, nourishment makes them strong and large enough to return upstream to their birth habitats; their bodies bring munificent nourishment from the sea to enrich their birth habitats; a new generation of fry finds its nourishment in the sea-enriched inland habitat; and so on. These days, ecological loops and intersecting loops are constantly being identified and measured. But there's a sad and desperate reason for so much interest. We're cutting such loops at a terrible rate. Well, at least knowing what we're doing wrong is one prerequisite to doing better."

"It's impossible to imagine how either ecosystems or economies could fend off collapse in the absence of beneficent loops," said Hiram. "Positive-feedback loops are the very structure, the very context, within which bifurcations and diversity can emerge; positive-feedback loops permit biomass expansion and economic expansion without loss of dynamic stability; in fact, they enhance both dynamism and stability."

"Why do you say 'feedback loops'?" asked Hortense.

"What does feedback have to do with this? Straighten me out."

"Feedback refers to information regarding a system that the system both reports and responds to. The information can be carried by any medium—monetary, demographic, mechanical, chemical, electrical, whatever. The feedback triggers an effective response to its information.

"In digital systems, electrically carried information activates switches that have only two positions: on or off—that is, positive or negative positions."

"Doesn't that have to do with cybernetics?" asked Armbruster, adding, "*Kybernetes* is Greek for 'steersman.' "

"A splendid word for the workings of feedback," said Hiram, "with its image of a hand on the tiller, keeping a vessel on course. It was coined by Norbert Wiener, one of the brilliant founders of computer science. The terms *positive feedback* and *negative feedback* make sense for electronic circuits. They've oozed into the language as generalized terms for feedback in systems where *positive* and *negative* are far-fetched and even confusing. A good way to distinguish which feedback is which is to remember that positive responses reinforce or intensify what the feedback is reporting. Negative feedback, which I'll take up later, works entirely differently because negative responses cancel—negate—what the feedback is reporting."

"Folk etymology to the rescue," said Armbruster. "I've always had trouble remembering which is which. Positive-feedback loops are marvelous, Hiram; so much less upsetting and problematic than bifurcations."

"Wait," said Hiram. "Positive feedback is treacherous. Remember that responses to it intensify and reinforce. They can intensify unstable or otherwise destructive situ-

ations as automatically and reliably as they intensify stabilizing and constructive situations. Then we call the loops
vicious circles. For instance, suppose that an animal falls
sick or is wounded and thus becomes incapable of finding
food for the time being. Lack of food further weakens the
animal; it becomes even less capable of finding food; so it
further weakens; and so on. Even if it isn't put out of its
misery by a predator, that malign loop ends in the animal's
death, its collapse. In this case, a formerly benign self-
refueling loop has gone into reverse, even though it still
operates as a positive response, a reinforcing response, to
the new situation the feedback reports."

"Here's a common economic example," said Murray.
"Feedback reports that operating income isn't sufficient to
cover operating expenses. Suppose the response is to ob-
tain a loan to make up the discrepancy. The loan itself adds
interest costs to operating expenses. That increases the discrepancy. Therefore, still more money is borrowed. That
increases the discrepancy further, and so on. This vicious
circle is called deficit financing, and finally it becomes fi-
nancially insupportable."

"Vicious circles are dead ends, because instead of correcting an instability reported by the system, they intensify
it," said Hiram. "The area of the North Atlantic off Newfoundland, called the Grand Banks, supported fishermen
and their communities and supplied food to Europeans
and North Americans for more than three centuries. The
cod seemed inexhaustible as catches increased year after
year, averaging half a million tons annually during the first
half of the twentieth century. Then soaring rapidly,
catches reached three times that amount annually during
the late 1960s.

"After that, catches began to decline and the size of individual fish to decrease, and cod prices rose. The international fishing industry responded to the feedback on creeping scarcity and rising prices by investing in larger fishing trawlers and bigger nets. When catches rapidly diminished further, the response was to comb the sea with still bigger and more efficient nets, and so on, until the Grand Banks cod fishery utterly collapsed in 1992. No more cod. This was a horrendous economic and social disaster for Newfoundland fishermen and fish-plant workers and their communities, to say nothing of an ecological disaster, whose ramifications are still unknown."

"The trouble wasn't the feedback information but the response to it," said Kate. "The correct response would have been to let up on catches when they started to diminish. What the fishermen did was illogical."

"Some fisheries scientists and ecologists advised letting up," said Hiram. "So did some of the fishermen—those who used small boats and nets in waters close to shore—when they noticed that the cod they caught were getting smaller. The inshore fishermen, as they're called, were alarmed and outraged by the big trawlers and huge nets farther out. But neither inshore fishermen nor ecologists swung weight with the Canadian or Newfoundland government or the international fishing industry."

"By its own lights, Kate, the industry was responding logically," said Murray. "Larger boats and bigger nets were a big investment. Paying off bigger capital costs added to the pressure to fish diligently."

"Vicious circles and their ultimately futile costs aren't necessarily clear while they're in the making," said Hiram. "Take this example. During rush hour, some roads became congested, the information fed back in the form of traffic jams and longer travel times. On the one hand, this could logically be taken to mean that cars and trucks were being depended upon too heavily and that alternate means were needed to help move people and goods—or perhaps that unnecessary transport was overburdening the system because zoning regulations separated everyday conveniences and work from residences. But on the other hand, congestion could as logically be taken to mean that existing roads and streets were inadequate, in which case a logical response was to widen streets and build more roads.

"The second of these two possible responses won out. But since bigger and better roads and faster speeds on them encouraged more use of cars and also greater numbers of cars, congestion built up again, requiring more street widening, more roads, more highways, more parking spaces, and so on. The result of enormous expenditures and effort has been that cars still crawl at some twelve miles an hour during lengthening rush hours.

"This road-traffic vicious circle is intersected and intensified by others. The car–suburban sprawl vicious circle makes transit routes expensive and otherwise impractical; therefore, cars are even more necessary; therefore people who can't afford cars are required to support them regardless, intensifying the road-traffic loop. It's also intensified by the falling-transit-ridership and falling-transit-service loop. As riders and fare incomes drop, transit services are reduced; therefore, more riders and fares are lost; therefore, service is further reduced; and so on—to the point of collapse, meaning the disappearance of former transit services."

"Except for the animal that progressively grows too weak or sick to find nourishment for itself, all your examples of vicious circles are owing to greed or mistaken logic," said Armbruster. "Doesn't the rest of nature generate vicious circles without aid from us?"

"Vicious circles are damaging but self-terminating," said Hiram. "Even the road-traffic loop can't continue intensifying indefinitely. When vicious circles appear in the rest of nature, which is less given to temporizing with them than we are, they vanish, because they self-destruct like the sick animal.

"However, the fact of ice ages, which have occurred in geologic time, suggests great and portentous vicious circles. Here's one hypothetical, simplified scenario: Atmospheric warming, caused by gases or particles that capture heat from the sun, might increase precipitation at the comparatively cold poles. That would enlarge ice caps and glaciers, which reflect heat instead of absorbing it; therefore cold would deepen; therefore ice would spread further; and so on. Add an intersecting vicious circle caused by the decrease in heat-absorbing biomass, and you get an idea of the possible workings of vicious circles on a grand scale. Theorists have constructed various differing scenarios, necessarily all speculative. But the facts are that ice ages have recurred, something must cause them, and they can't be accounted for by more direct causes, such as alterations in the sun's output of energy or in the earth's orbit. One scientist, the atmospheric chemist James Lovelock—who propounded the Gaia Theory you asked about, Hortense—thinks that ice ages are the normal condition for the planet and that warm, interglacial periods such as the one we now enjoy are the aberrations to be accounted for. If he's right, it would be normal for Siberia, Scandinavia, Canada, and perhaps where we're sitting right now to be under ice."

Everybody sat in glum silence until Armbruster spoke

up. "Economic vicious circles—have we any way of protecting ourselves from them? There seems to be a missing link here in the combat against collapse."

"Economic vicious circles tend to be subsidized," said Hiram. "If not at first, then soon, and ever more heavily as time passes. We could keep them in hand—at least theoretically—if they had to pay their costs and include those in prices."

"But I thought you said costs of boats and nets, and rising prices of cod, helped drive that vicious circle," protested Hortense.

"I neglected to mention that the cod fishery and its workers were subsidized—in Canada, ever more heavily during the years cod were declining. Had it been possible to add subsidy costs into cod prices, cod would have priced itself out of the market before fish stocks collapsed. Subsidies were intended to support the industry and its workers, and they did. The price of automobiles doesn't begin to pay for their many indirect costs: waste of land and energy, loss of amenities, and the expenses of traffic enforcement, pollution, and accidents caused by uninsured drivers.

"I suppose what I'm saying is this: Economic vicious circles are intended to solve problems, but they don't. The problems they're meant to solve persist; as solutions recede, the costs of temporizing continue to rise. We should become suspicious of activities displaying these characteristics and seek to cut vicious circles instead of indulging them—essentially the same advice given drug abusers, compulsive gamblers, smokers, or other addicts. Economic vicious circles are economic and political addictions. The most effective ways to cut them are with bifurcations instead of continuing as is.

"Please notice that both benign feedback loops and vicious circles reach limits. Redwood trees don't grow into the stratosphere and pine trees don't grow as tall as redwoods, even though they benefit from their own height-fog loops. To take an economic example, a city that replaces and shifts imports repeatedly doesn't aggrandize the economy of the whole world."

"I can understand that the trees have genetic and mechanical limits," said Hortense. "But do import-replacing, import-shifting cities also have limits?"

"They do, because other cities with beneficent loops at work are also replacing and shifting imports and thus are subtracting exports from each other. Therefore, a city that has already achieved a large and diverse economy must continue to replace imports merely to maintain its economy and compensate for its losses. In other words, beneficent loops operate to achieve stability up to their limit; from that point on, they act to maintain stability, but they're still as necessary as before. The system must still continue to be dynamic or it will deteriorate.

"A vicious circle's limit is not an achieved dynamic equilibrium but collapse. It dead-ends. The debt becomes insupportable. The fishery collapses. The transit system disappears. The compulsive gambler runs out of funds or embezzles. Vicious circles run their self-destructive course and vanish."

With an air of having nothing more to say on the subject, Hiram took a drink of mineral water and changed his jacket for a sweater Hortense had hung over the arm of his chair.

"I don't know that I really want to hear about other self-corrections for instabilities, considering how they can turn around and bite you," said Armbruster. "But let's be brave and push on. What's your next category, Hiram? I think you said negative feedback."

"Yes, but continue to be cheered by positive-feedback loops in spite of their betrayals," said Hiram. "Beneficent ones are still at work in both ecosystems and economies."

"How can you be sure?" asked Hortense.

"Otherwise the world would be dead. You'll like negative-feedback controls, Armbruster. Here's where Norbert Wiener's image of a steersman with his hand on the tiller—and his eye on the compass—is especially apt.

"Our own routine breathing illustrates the principle. We know when it's time to take another breath, because a rise in the level of carbon dioxide in the bloodstream automatically triggers the brain stem's breathing center to shoot a message to the diaphragm to contract and allow the lungs to fill with another breath. A deviation from a predetermined standard is being corrected in this case."

"Last week the paper reported that laboratory rats know when to eat," said Armbruster, "because when energy carried in the bloodstream drops below a certain level, the information automatically triggers the brain to produce a chemical that makes the animal want to eat. The chemical's been named orexin, from the Greek for 'hunger.' The item interested me because my weight tends to get out of hand."

"Our bodies contain immense arrays of negative-feedback controls," said Hiram. "They help regulate the work of our immune, digestive, metabolic, muscular, reproductive, and nervous systems, our ability to repair ourselves, the senses with which we interpret the world—all our bodily functions. Biologists keep discovering them. We ourselves aren't aware of them."

"Descartes might better have said, 'I *don't* think, therefore I am,' " chuckled Armbruster.

"Conscious thinking, unconscious thinking, and not thinking all share responsibility for the astonishing fact 'I am,' " said Kate.

"In ecosystems, negative-feedback controls restore balances between predators and prey," said Hiram.

"Now you're laboring the obvious," said Armbruster. "I think we all understand that if the population of rabbits increases, so does the population of foxes. I don't mean to complain, but I'm anxious for us to get on with economies."

"Obvious this may be," said Hiram, "but ponder the complexity of an ecosystem with its feedback messages racing inside plants and animals, and among animals that have relationships with one another, the responses racing back and forth, and the responses themselves feeding into the ecosystem as feedback information. Such volatility, such intricacy, such self-organization! Then think of the dynamic order an ecosystem imposes on itself, and think about the dynamic order our own bodies impose on themselves unbeknownst to us, intimate as we are with them. Such thoughts can help you appreciate the dynamic order that a complicated economy also imposes on itself."

As Hiram paused, Hortense broke in, with an apologetic smile for Armbruster. "I'm absolutely starved. We've run on, and it's already afternoon, high time for—"

"Look!" cried Kate, pointing to a window. Absorbed as they were, no one had noticed how black the sky had become. While Kate was still pointing, the window rattled, lightning zigzagged, thunder boomed, the clouds burst. Without a word, all five of them jumped up and rushed about, shutting windows. Hiram took longest, checking his tenants' apartments. Once he returned, he motioned everyone into the adjoining dining room. "Here's where we'll have our picnic," he said.

Hortense, who used the dining room as her makeshift study, hastily cleared the table of books and papers, piling them neatly on the floor in a corner. Armbruster spied a baseboard outlet and plugged in his recorder. Murray produced a tablecloth from the sideboard and brought in two picnic baskets and a thermos jug from the kitchen. Kate opened a basket and stacked sandwiches on two paper plates, while Hiram found the paper cups, poured lemonade, and opened a pickle jar. Hortense, placing candles on the table, said, "Let's pretend the storm cut off the electricity."

Helping himself to a corned-beef-and-watercress sandwich on rye, Armbruster said to Hiram, "You were just leading up to money feedback, if I'm not mistaken."

Hiram, nodding, reluctantly set down a forkful of potato salad. "Adam Smith, back in 1775, identified prices of goods and rates of wages as feedback information, although of course he didn't call it that because the word *feedback* was not in the vocabulary at the time. But he understood the idea. He analyzed how prices automatically corrected maladjustments between supply and demand. It was not, he found, by merely influencing distribution of supplies—that was an old piece of knowledge—but by actually bringing imbalances into better balance by triggering changes in production. In his sober way, Smith was clearly excited about the marvelous form of order he'd discovered, as well he should have been. He was far ahead of naturalists in grasping the principle of negative-feedback controls. Even machine designers didn't recognize that they were dealing with—"

"Please stay on the subject of money," said Armbruster. "What does machine design have to do with this?"

"Oh, lots of machines incorporate negative-feedback controls. Thermostats register temperature feedback and trigger corrective responses by heat sources. Or take the flywheel, an early mechanical example—" Registering Armbruster's frown as feedback information, Hiram quickly got back on course. "It's interesting, I think, that Smith visualized negative economic feedback control as a hidden hand ordering the market, and some two centuries later Wiener visualized feedback as a hand on a rudder." Hiram reached for his fork again, thought better of it, and pushed away his plate.

"Hiram, you go ahead and eat," said Murray. "I can talk on this subject. Adam Smith observed that prices rise for goods in short supply and fall for goods in low demand."

"Like outlet stores advertising sale prices on manufacturers' overstocks, I suppose," said Hortense.

"That kind of thing is feedback. Now, for corrections it triggers," Murray went on. "Smith also observed that high prices for goods stimulated increased production of those goods and that low prices depressed production, automatically bringing supplies into closer correspondence with demand. He also applied this insight to facets of economic life other than production of goods. For instance, he noticed that wages rise when and where the demand for labor is high and fall when and where it's in low demand. This influences migrations of workers when such movements are possible, and also workers' choices of occupations when that's feasible. When and where capital is in high demand, interest rates rise and attract capital.

"Such continual adjustments—by industry, labor, customers, landowners, and capital—create self-organized order out of volatile, uncoordinated, confusing conglomerations of countless different enterprises and individuals, narrowly pursuing countless picayune opportunities and their own interests. So Smith was also far ahead of his time in identifying the phenomenon we now call self-organization and illustrating its behavior in a nonhierarchically organized, dynamic system.

"Smith shared with his contemporaries many naive and obfuscating misconceptions about the world and the way it works. Nevertheless, these insights of his placed economics, in 1775, at a forefront of scientific inquiry. No wonder early ecologists drew on economics to explain their own discoveries.

"Unfortunately, economics failed to progress much further as a science. It had this one solid concept in its grasp, and economists and economic philosophers tried to make it explain too much. They dwelled on arid arguments about whether supply generates demand or demand generates supply—arguments that continue to this day.

"As we've seen, diversity generates economic expansion, owing to multiple reuses of settlements' imports, in principle just as diversity of organisms generates biomass expansion owing to multiple reuses of received energy before it leaves the conduit. But although the close empiric connection between economic diversity and expansion was observable in Smith's time and has been observable ever since, the connection slid unnoticed past economic theorists arrested in their obsession with whether demand leads supply or vice versa. Smith himself was partly responsible for that blind spot. He led himself and others astray by declaring that economic specialization of regions and nations was more efficient than economic diversification; his mistake came of flawed assumptions and extrapolations concerning division of labor.

"To this day, no attention is paid to self-refueling as a complex but orderly process. And only in the mid-twentieth century did schools of economics so much as acknowledge that innovation—development—was worth exploring, and even then only as an eccentric and marginal side issue. And even today there is no useful attention paid to the systematic workings of development and co-development. The pity is that this intellectual stultification was so unnecessary . . ." Murray's voice trailed off.

"Why unnecessary?" asked Armbruster. "Keep explaining."

"The theorists after Smith retreated into their own heads instead of engaging ever more deeply with the real world. Plenty of observable, germane facts were lying around in plain sight, ready and waiting to lead Smith's insights, straight as directional arrows, into the subjects of development and bifurcations. It could easily have been seen by anyone, for instance, that high prices stimulate substitutes for goods in short supply—that is, stimulate production of goods not previously in existence. In fifteenth-century Europe, the demand for books exceeded the supply of individually hand-copied books. That particular imbalance made printing with movable type economically feasible. Printed books were not only more plentiful than hand copies but cheaper than even those produced by poor, half-starved student drudges in cold, ill-lit garrets.

"Or take metal plating, an important industrial advance even before Smith's time and observable in many permutations ever since. The innovation that launched it in London was a lower-priced substitute for sterling-silver handles for table knives. In both printing and plating—and many other instances—disparate supplies and demands were brought into better balance only by developments."

"But don't forget, those developments couldn't have been undertaken without co-developments," said Kate.

"Yes, thank you, Kate. Pursuing Smith's insights could have led straight into appreciation of co-development webs and would have thrown deep suspicion on economic specialization—and also on the supposed efficiency of monopolies, and on the deliberately specialized economic arrangements of imperial powers, which have worked so much harm on the world's economies and the people who depend on them.

"As for refueling, London, for one, was subject to enormous bursts of replacements of former imports; so were other European cities. Since these replacements were largely—not entirely, but largely—driven by the lower costs of locating close to markets instead of at a distance, Smith's insights might have led to understanding why some economies, by diversifying, also become self-generating while others are dependent and inert.

"All these investigations would have been more fruitful than theories about how economies should work or might work or could be manipulated into how they should or might work—instead of learning how they do work. What a waste.

"But as far as negative-feedback control is concerned, Smith was brilliant. He realized that feedback is only as good as the accuracy of its reporting. He identified combines to rig prices as falsifications of realities about supply and demand. He saw that false information injected disorder into the system he was observing and describing."

Hiram, who had finished eating, said, "Your turn to have

lunch, Pop. Let me pick up on how feedback can be true, false, or ambiguous. Negative-feedback controls are most reliable when the data reported, the purport of the data, and the corrective response are functionally integrated so there is no possibility of misunderstanding the information or triggering a mistaken response.

"For programmed feedback-control perfection, there are few better places to look than colonies of social insects. For example, a termite colony maintains balanced proportions among its different castes. They're all born of identical eggs with exactly the same genetic heredity, yet the adults greatly differ physically, depending on the functions they perform. The nursery of the larvae is where such differences are determined, by cascades of chemicals activated in the larvae by feedback reported as information on current populations of the various castes in the colony. For instance, a colony's soldiers give off an odor, a pheromone distinctive to the soldiers. If the odor falls below a certain level in the colony, it means that the proportion of soldiers is less than normal; there's no mistaking the purport of the feedback. Since the drop automatically causes the nursery to supply more soldiers, there's no room for mistake in the response—or in cessation of the response, either. Pheromone feedback from newly produced soldiers reports, 'That's enough soldiers.' In short, data, the meaning of the data, and appropriate responses to the data are all perfectly integrated. Most negative-feedback controls, including most of those that operate within our own bodies, have comparable integral perfection."

"I don't want to prolong your detour into natural history," said Armbruster, "but I feel bound to point out, Hiram, that nature's feedback reports can be false and the lies can be damaging. Spells of warm weather in midwinter

aren't unknown. But if plants take that data on temperature to mean that spring has come, they're nipped in the
bud."

"A good illustration of data and its purport not being integrated," said Hiram. "But it's surprising and gratifying to
see how seldom native plants are fatally fooled. Their protection is their sensitivity to multiple reports. If data on
temperature contradict data on length of the day, the temperature data are apparently suspect."

"If plants are smart enough to take multiple messages
into account, we should be smart enough, too," said Kate.
"Remember, you pointed out that automotive traffic congestion could logically be taken to mean either that more
and wider roads are needed or that automobiles and trucks
are too heavily depended on to move people and goods.
However, messages of so many different kinds eventually
come in that more and wider roads aren't solving congestion—and yet we keep on behaving as if they do. So it's
pointless for us to blame the initial ambiguity of feedback
messages about traffic for our own heedlessness to later
clarifications."

"Please, not another detour into that tiresome vicious
circle," said Armbruster. "Give us more on price feedback."

"Price feedback is inherently well integrated," said
Hiram. "It's not sloppy, not ambiguous. As Smith per-
ceived, the data carry meaningful information on imbalances of supply and demand and they do automatically
trigger corrective responses. So data and its purport and
responses are all of a piece. But—and this is a very big
but—the data themselves, prices, can be false, and of
course that makes the inherent integrity count for nothing—go haywire."

"Costs are a major ingredient of prices," Murray put in.

"Costs can be falsified, and if so, then prices will be falsified too."

"Yes, subsidies falsify both costs and prices," said Hiram. "And as I indicated in passing earlier, lies of that sort warp development."

"As if printing was an economic failure because hand-copied manuscripts were too heavily subsidized by monasteries," said Hortense. "I suppose that's an idiotic suggestion—"

"Not idiotic in principle," said Hiram. "In addition to subsidies, there are many other ways to falsify costs and prices. Taxes are significant costs, and tax policies can favor some types of investment and production and penalize others. Tariffs falsify prices; that's their purpose. Speculative bubbles falsify prices by injecting wishful thinking, based on nothing but contagions of wishful thinking, which is why bubble prices collapse when more solid realities eventually catch up with them. Kickbacks and bribes falsify honest costs.

"An oddity of the Soviet economic system was that the costs of most production and services were unknown. Really unknown. Managers of factories, offices, farms, mines, hospitals, theaters, whatever—they literally did not know the costs of what they were producing. Budgets existed, to be sure—allocations for expenses—but these were so infused and confused by subsidies that they bore little or no relation to actual costs. Cost accounting didn't matter in any case, because prices were fixed by edict. Feedback controls were expunged from economic life except on the black market, where they tended to pop up irrepressibly.

"The most pervasive and tenacious falsifications of costs and prices tend to be imposed institutionally," Hiram went on. "Other aims of political or social institutions take priority over accuracy of costs and prices. The Soviet economic system was an extreme example of this institutional tendency."

"But the successor economy in post-Soviet Russia is as cavalier about costs and prices for quite different reasons," said Murray. "Change in the political system there hasn't restored price feedback controls. Russian enterprises still ignore cost accounting. Their people don't know how to do it, and they don't seem to learn, because they evidently don't understand its importance as guidance to what they're doing well and what they're doing badly. Monopolies, established by cronyism and strong-arm methods, along with pervasive extortion and corruption, falsify actual costs anyhow; racketeering entrepreneurs prefer eliminating competitors to competing with them on prices, quality, and service. What's all the more sickening is that this economic mess and its terrible poverty are mixed with sentimental longings for a Mother Russia who will take care of her good children if they revert to simple peasant communal virtues. From what I hear, the Ukrainian economy is even more rickety. These are economies still far removed from making continual, subtle, automatic corrections in what they produce, and where and how."

"I didn't finish with institutionalized price falsifications," said Hiram. "Here's one more example: Rises and declines in the relative value of national currencies should theoretically give valuable and corrective feedback on international trade. Falling currency values make exports cheaper and imports more expensive. That should stimulate a nation's international exports, and also its replacements of imports—precisely when a drop in currency value reports that these corrections to trade imbalances are needed. But as the great import-substitution fiasco demonstrated so well, corrections of this kind are specific to localities. Except in cases of very small countries—in effect, city-states—national currencies blur conglomerations of many different localities and their varied trade needs and possibilities; and besides that, national currencies yield no feedback on trade imbalances within a nation. Pegged currencies and speculative trade in currencies contribute still more disorder.

"In sum, Smith's 'invisible hand' of the market labors under many grave disabilities. Yet even so, it does labor on automatically and tirelessly where it isn't forestalled."

Murray, who had merely picked at his food, said abruptly, "Let's go into the living room, where the chairs are more comfortable." The rain had stopped and the sun returned, but outdoors everything was still soaked and dripping. Back the group trooped to the living room, Armbruster with his recorder in hand.

Once they were settled with coffee and fruit, Armbruster said, "I'm braced now for bad news about negative-feedback controls. The shortcomings you've mentioned so far aren't flaws of these stabilizers themselves but the result of people gumming up the data. Now, tell us how they themselves turn nasty on us."

"Their usual chief virtue, which is a reliable, robotic nature, is also their chief occasional flaw," said Hiram. "But in most instances, evolution overcomes that flaw. Again, our breathing can serve as illustration. What if you fall into water? If you had nothing but the automatic breathing response I described, its robotic reliability would kill you. However, a different part of your brain can countermand the brain stem's order to the diaphragm—can tell the diaphragm, 'Hold it!' This contradiction to the robot in us can't last long, but in spite of its brevity, the ability to contradict is vital. Furthermore, we contradict routine breathing control to satisfy other purposes. We can't breathe and swallow at the same time without choking, and we make the robot steersman accommodate to that. If we didn't have an edge of discretionary control, we couldn't talk, sing, or blow out a candle.

"Armbruster, you mentioned that it's hard for you to keep your weight in hand. When the robot in you reports that you've had enough, another part of your brain says, 'Don't stop.' Hey, don't look at me as if I've caught you with your hand in the cookie jar! It's useful to be able to stuff yourself opportunistically, hungry or not, if you aren't sure when you'll eat next—which must often have been a state that our remote, and not so remote, ancestors were in."

"Animals have discretion, too," said Kate. "Suppose a hungry rabbit, its brain awash in orexin, becomes aware of an eagle; it stops hopping and nibbling and freezes to wait out the danger. Maybe terror automatically makes the rabbit lose its appetite, but in any event—"

"In any event, a special threat required a special response out of the routine, to fit the situation," Hiram finished her thought.

"Then why not just say that dynamic systems benefit from routine behavior when that is stabilizing and flexible behavior when routine behavior isn't appropriate?" asked Armbruster.

"Too vague," said Hiram. "Suppose the rabbit trying to escape the attention of the eagle didn't freeze but instead began frantically digging a burrow in which to hide. That would demonstrate an admirable degree of flexibility. But what a mistake!

"We're talking now about emergency adaptations to address temporary instabilities—the fourth category of corrections. This category isn't a catchall of leftover random responses, although at first thought it may seem so. Rather, it speaks of instabilities that are only temporary but may nevertheless be devastating. Again, evolution provides answers to many such threats of collapse. For instance, in temperate ecosystems some organisms hibernate, some spin cocoons, some lose foliage, and so on—all of which are adaptations to winter."

"But those are normal parts of normal life cycles," said Kate.

"True, but they are also adaptations to circumvent dire threats appearing seasonally. Besides those, abnormal vicissitudes pose abnormal threats. Examples are prolonged droughts, hurricanes, abnormal floods, ice storms, fires set by lightning in unusually rapid succession, plant and animal diseases, and invasions of alien species with no native predators to keep them in check. Unusual vicissitudes result in striking differences in survival rates among organisms in ecosystems. Organisms equipped to adapt to them do best, of course.

"This is more fanciful than I like to be," Hiram went on. "But we can make an analogy between seasonal cycles and normal business cycles. Both can be expected—the business cycles possibly because of irregular rates at which settlements refuel, diversify, and expand, although that's speculation. At any rate, business cycles, like winter, recur often enough to be expected. Though they're harsh, economies can adapt to them reasonably well by preparing in advance—if they can afford it—with unemployment insurance, means of protecting bankrupt enterprises and individuals temporarily from their creditors, measures for safeguarding people's pensions and savings, welfare assistance, and charitable help.

"But great economic depressions and wars are another matter. Partly because they can threaten the stability of the state as well as the economy, and also because they may not be anticipated, they require swift and extraordinary adaptations. I'm almost afraid to say this, for fear you'll assume I'm trivializing wars and depressions, but the kinds of measures these require—speedy, improvisational—are in the same category as our speedy, improvisational responses when the cloudburst forced a sudden change in our lunch plans."

"You're describing patterns," said Kate.

"Yes. Whatever the situation seems to require at the moment is tried. If it seems to work, it's adopted. People plunge into activities they didn't contemplate doing. Money that wasn't budgeted is spent. Goods may be rationed, prices fixed, some projects and plans unceremoniously halted and others hastily embraced—whatever it takes. If all that can be done isn't enough, the system collapses.

"Our bodies combat onslaughts of infectious diseases with extraordinary emergency measures, such as fever—abnormal temperature, sometimes so high that it is fatal in itself if it's sustained very long. Killer cells of the immune system swiftly multiply by the millions to battle the infecting organisms. If all the strength that a sick individual can marshal is needed for the emergency, other tasks of life are simply abandoned for the time being. But a healthy organism, having survived such a crisis, doesn't keep running a fever or abandon interest in either the sensual pleasures or the vexations of life."

"Crisis behavior is damaging except in times of crisis," said Kate. "For instance, in autoimmune diseases, such as painful, crippling arthritis, a person's killer cells fail to distinguish between harmful invaders and the body's 'self.'

They attack without reason to attack. At least, that's the current theory."

"Armbruster, do you remember that I mentioned overeating as a useful adaptation to uncertainty?" asked Hiram. "If the adaptation hangs on when it's no longer needed, it's anachronistic. Anachronistic adaptations are the hidden traps in urgency or emergency adaptations. Monopolies, justifiable in some instances on grounds of urgency, hang on anachronistically and become drags and stultifiers. Farm subsidies were instituted in the 1930s to save family farms in the Great Depression; then, as anachronisms, permanent and bloated, they disproportionately rewarded large-scale factory farming—ironically, to the disadvantage of smaller-scale family farming. New York City failed to abandon rent controls instituted after civilian construction was halted during the Second World War; then, as anachronisms, ironically, rent controls depressed construction. Armament manufacturing soars during wars, of course; if it remains anachronistically inflated, producers seek wars, arms smugglers, and civilian customers for assault guns and ammunition."

Murray spoke up. "During the Great Depression, the English economist John Maynard Keynes proposed that governments compensate for bank credit which had dried up by undertaking their own investment programs and that they compensate for lack of individuals' purchasing power by transfer payments. Keynes was a demand-side economist, meaning he believed demand leads supply to generate economic activity and expansion. His idea was that governments could even out economic instabilities by means of deficit financing in hard times and debt-reducing budget surpluses in good times. In effect, he was trying to invent a new negative-feedback control, which he hoped would keep the vessel on course. Many governments did adopt deficit financing for hard times, but then anachronistically they hung on to it, good times or bad, creating the vicious circle of intractable indebtedness that I mentioned earlier today."

"And business cycles, with accompanying unemployment, recurred anyway, as mysteriously as ever," said Hiram, "regardless of attempts to eliminate them with Keynes's prescription. Eventually, Keynes himself, gloomily observing Britain's economic decline, speculated that economies might be subject to deeper 'structural' flaws, as he called them, meaning flaws apparently not subject to correction by monetary, budgetary, and tax manipulations.

"Of course, economies in which settlements aren't developing, diversifying, and self-refueling are loaded with economic flaws. Nothing can cure such flaws except settlements that develop, diversify, and refuel. Murray, do you think—"

Hiram fell silent. Murray, his head propped on his palm, was asleep in his comfortable chair, starting to snore gently.

"He usually takes an afternoon nap," Hiram whispered.

"Don't wake him," said Hortense softly. She pointed to the dining room and tiptoed her way in, and the rest of them followed. Armbruster unplugged his machine and transported it yet again, closing the door quietly behind him.

Chapter 6

THE DOUBLE NATURE OF

FITNESS FOR SURVIVAL

"Now what?" asked Armbruster. "Should we continue without Murray, or should we take a recess?"

"Kate mentioned that she had something to contribute," said Hortense.

Without waiting for permission or agreement, Kate seized the opening Hortense had given her. "I've been thinking about fitness for survival in ecosystems. And do be patient with me, Armbruster, because this is relevant to economic life. Fitness as determined by natural selection means that an organism is successful in competing to feed and breed. It also means that the organism must have traits which prevent it from destroying its own habitat, because an indispensable requirement for the organism is an arena in which to feed, breed, and compete.

"In this light," she went on, "consider the great cats: If they were so inclined, they could wipe out all their prey, then starve. Yet a gazelle or two at a time is enough for them. I once took a house cat into an abandoned apartment where quite a bit of food had been left. As you would expect, it was overrun with mice. They were even in the refrigerator, and to my amazement, when I looked in the freezer compartment, they were scampering across ice cubes and gnawing frozen foods. When I opened cupboard doors and disturbed them, mice ran about everywhere. Although the cat had been fed and wasn't hungry, it went for the mice with gusto. However, after catching only three, it goofed off for the rest of the day on a sunny windowsill while I dumped food into garbage bags, swept up, and then set traps.

"The great jungle cats share the same trait as that house cat. Prudence doesn't restrain them from unremitting killing, as far as we can tell. The check seems to be their disposition to snooze and bask instead of exerting themselves unnecessarily.

"Elephants uproot and trample impressive swaths as they feed and wander. If they were so inclined, they could convert their own habitats to desert—to their own disadvantage. But they're drawn to other occupations, such as playing in rivers, squirting themselves and each other with water, and milling about sociably on land, evidently finding interest and contentment in each other's company.

"Bonobos, the recently famous primates that are one of our two closest living cousin species, are celebrated—or notorious—for the time and effort they devote to sex play totally unrelated to reproducing. Our other close relatives, the chimpanzees, go in for grooming each other like workaholic nursemaids or demented hairdressers in the ample time they take off from exploiting their habitats. One could go on and on: Otters play on water slides; raccoons gambol and roll about together—evolution has equipped them with things to do other than catching all the fish available or otherwise tearing apart their habitats."

"Time out from nature red in tooth and claw," said Armbruster.

"I've heard that bluefish kill without letup," said Hortense. "But of course the ocean is too big to be destroyed by them."

Hiram looked skeptical. "Those traits you mention may simply enhance competitive natural selection," he said. "The great cats could be aiding digestion with their lazy ways, and rejuvenating stressed muscles. Elephants have to cool down or their own body heat would kill them. Bonobos' and chimpanzees' capers maintain their troops' social structures. Otters' and raccoons' games could keep them alert and in trim."

"An organ or a form of behavior often serves several different purposes simultaneously," said Kate.

"What about ants and bees?" asked Hortense. "Their worker castes are busy, busy, busy. No time out for them—nor for their egg-laying factories, the queens."

"The diligence of bees and ants is habitat-enhancing, not habitat-destroying," said Kate. "You could say the same about the beneficial bacteria in our guts and the symbiotic descendants of bacteria in our cells. On the other hand, a bacterium that kills off its host—before it has a chance to infect another host—kills itself off."

"But as a rule," said Hiram, "evolution equips some of a lethal bacterium's hosts with a mutation that renders the bacterium merely debilitating or even innocuous, and those are the hosts that survive and multiply."

"The most successful predators, large or small, are the ones that graduate to become symbionts in their habitats," said Kate.

"What about plants?" asked Armbruster. "Vines could smother everything—like kudzu, which has strayed out of

Asia and is now smothering entire forests in Alabama. In those habitats, kudzu can reign supreme forever, unless human beings get it under control."

"No it can't," said Kate. "It looks successful now, but it's destroying the very habitats in which it seems to have won the prize for fitness. It's living on already accumulated, complex richness in the soil. That's evident from the fact that you don't find kudzu growing on bare rocks or in sterile clay. All plants, like all animals, need communities of other organisms. No one kind of plant extracts from rock or soil everything it requires, including minute quantities of trace elements."

"In other words, you're saying that kudzu in an Alabama shrub land or forest has trapped itself in a vicious circle," said Armbruster. "The more successful it is at squelching other plants, the more it must draw on previously accumulated capital in the soil, leaving less for other plants, and so on. Finally, the capital runs out and the kudzu with it."

"Unless evolution makes it less lethal to its habitat and hence to itself," said Hiram.

"I'm proposing that fitness for survival by natural selection has two faces," said Kate. "The two are equally important. One is competitive success at feeding and breeding. This accounts for natural selection by survival of the fittest according to conventional evolutionary theory. Modern evolutionists have added to this concept the accidents of good and bad luck. The extreme version of the theory of fitness determined by competitive success at breeding is the 'selfish gene'—the view that genes are directed by their competitive drive to survive and propagate and that an organism carrying the genes is merely a vehicle for furthering the competitive drive of its genes.

"I'm suggesting this view is too simple. So was Darwin's

own narrowing of success to competitive success. It doesn't take into account evolutionary success at habitat maintenance. Both the competition and the arena for competition are necessary. Both those faces of fitness by natural selection must work in harmony. Neither can undermine the other; the penalty for that is unfitness to survive."

"Wait a minute," said Armbruster. "As Hiram said, one solution for a bacterium that's so lethal it destroys its own host before it infects another is for some of its hosts to develop resistance and multiply disproportionately. But that wouldn't be an internal check on the bacterium's potential for bringing itself to ruin."

"A host's resistance is a purely external check," Kate replied, "only if you write off the bacterium's own potential for becoming still more lethal. If it gives up on that arms race, it wins."

"So you're contending that habitat-preserving traits may look like losses in an arms race, or may seem to be frivolous and feckless, or, in the case of lions, sheer laziness, but that these traits can be important evolutionary assets if they help a species retain a viable habitat for itself. Sounds obvious when one thinks about it. Extinction from overweening success—is that possible?" Armbruster mused. "I wonder if that's what actually brought the big dinosaurs down while small dinosaurs, the ancestors of our birds, managed to survive, along with many unimpressive mammals, including our own ancestors. But why isn't fitness at habitat maintenance a major theme in the theory of natural selection by survival of the fittest?"

"I think I know why," said Hortense. "Human beings make up theories. Darwin lived in England in its heyday of empire building. His society idealized military virtues, masculine prowess, conquest, and hierarchical prestige.

I'm not saying that was Darwin's fault; it wasn't. But I'm saying that Darwin's social context rubbed off on his theory. Look at his identification of altruism with the willingness of soldiers to sacrifice their lives. That imposes an impossible evolutionary conundrum: Genes aren't transmitted by groups but by individuals; individuals lacking altruism as it was identified by Darwin would reproduce disproportionately by avoiding battle. Therefore, altruism clearly represents an unfit trait for reproductive success if you look for its root, or its extreme expression, in military service as Darwin did."

"Darwin realized that," said Hiram. "He deliberately drew attention to it as an unsolved puzzle. Neo-Darwinian evolutionists and evolutionary psychologists are still trying to solve the altruism puzzle by means of game models which show that altruism is self-interest or mathematical demonstrations which show that selfish genes further their own evolutionary interests by aiding survival of closely related genes in siblings and cousins."

"Darwin didn't seem to notice," said Hortense, "that in his very society, all around him, women bearing children were going into the equivalent of battle and doing it again and again, often making the ultimate sacrifice—their own lives. If one looks for altruism's extreme expression—self-sacrifice—in childbearing, altruism is no evolutionary puzzle. Individuals possessing the trait would reproduce disproportionately. The whole conundrum evaporates, simply doesn't exist."

The other three looked at Hortense in astonishment. "Hey, feminist evolution!" said Hiram.

"No, just plain straightforward evolution," said Hortense. "Peculiar only in not being skewed by masculinist evolution."

"But men are altruistic, too," said Armbruster. "How do you account for that?"

"Children inherit their nature from both parents," said Hortense. "In our species, the genders are much more alike than they're different. You might as well ask why men have nipples."

"What I'm pursuing," said Kate, "is the question of whether our species has inborn traits that restrain habitat destruction. On the one hand, it's plausible to think of our ruinous effects on the rest of nature as comparable to the kudzu vine's—smothering and plundering accumulated environmental riches, to our own eventual deterioration and destruction."

"Are you saying that we're doomed by the fact that our success as feeders and breeders is combined with heedless destructiveness to our habitation, the planet?" asked Hortense. "Oh dear, you sound like one more misanthropic ecologist."

"I'm not ready to concede any such thing," said Kate. "Think about habitats people have dwelled in and altered but haven't destroyed. Ask yourself, 'Why haven't they?' After all, people could have destroyed them. People have been capable destroyers for a long, long time. As soon as our species learned how to handle fire, and also invented effective hunting weapons and other foraging tools and techniques, it possessed effective means for ruining environments—ruining them heedlessly to no purpose or by exploiting them ruinously. That was possible, we know, because occasionally it did happen. The worst instances seem to have been widespread deforestation by fuel gatherers, followed by erosion, floods, abandonment of settlements, and impoverishment, or even disappearance of the offending societies. In other cases, herdsmen who mismanaged flocks allowed goats to convert shrub lands to desert. That's an example of new instabilities arising as unintended consequences of preceding bifurcations, Hiram. Sometimes hunters extinguished game, then moved on to extinguish more. Raiding and warfare included not only killing, looting, and enslaving but sometimes sheer destruction of enemy territory for vengeance or just for the hell of it. Scorched earth is not a modern invention. Romans knew how to destroy the enemy's habitat by sowing the land with salt. The great forests of the medieval Dalmatian coast, where are they now? Under water and muck, converted into the incredible pilings that support Venice but that left clear-cut mountains barren and rocky to this day."

"It's a wonder that anything's left," said Hortense.

"Isn't it?" said Kate. "And yet in most places, most of the time, people have managed to avoid destroying their habitats, including many they've occupied long and continuously. What could possibly have restrained our species? Something did, or else much of the earth, long, long since, would have been laid waste, then laid waste again as fast as it recovered—when it did recover. I'm speculating that our evolutionary endowments, like those of the great cats, elephants, bonobos, chimps, and others, must include traits that check habitat destruction."

"Don't keep us in suspense," said Hiram. "If you know what the saving traits are, tell us."

"No, of course I can't tell you. I can only speculate. But I have a few ideas. This is tricky stuff, because with human beings it's so hard to distinguish between inborn equipment and cultural practices. Here are my ground rules: Any restraints bestowed by evolution must cut across all cultures, over long spans of time, and must not be at odds with competitive success.

"One such trait is the capacity for aesthetic appreciation, which comes to us along with the evolutionary gift of consciousness. Evidence of aesthetic appreciation accompanies early evidences of Homo sapiens. Nobody who has seen reproductions of the most ancient cave paintings can doubt the aesthetic sensibility infusing them—no matter what other purposes they may or may not have served. Foragers have decorated themselves and their possessions, danced, and made music, all of which must have kept them from doing excessive foraging. Practicing and appreciating art is seldom environmentally harmful. It's especially significant, I think, that aesthetic appreciation includes admiration for the rest of nature: flowers, ocean waves, rocks, seashells, vines, human faces and figures, birds and other animals, the sun, the moon, stars, grasses, butterflies—recurring motifs in art, sometimes rendered literally, sometimes abstractly or formalized—and, in due course, art that shows appreciation of cultivated farmland, wild landscapes, seascapes, streetscapes, monuments, and domestic scenes."

"All true enough, but rather a weak reed to depend on," said Armbruster.

"No behavior so long lasting and universal can be deemed weak," said Kate. "From the arctic to the tropics, aesthetic appreciation is a human trait. If we found such persistent and widespread behavior in any other species, we'd assume it conferred an advantage of some kind—the way Hiram took it for granted that the laziness of the cats, the elephants' enjoyment of water play, and the capers of bonobos do. Why dismiss a persistent human trait as having no fitness advantage, or only a weak one? That's not a scientifically sound approach.

"Another trait, or rather pair of traits, that qualifies under my ground rules is fear of retribution for transgressions and the capacity to feel awe. Again, both are gifts of consciousness. In ancient times, offenders against the environment risked the fury of spirits of rivers, winds, volcanoes, the sea, forests. Wantonness could make animals disgruntled and malicious. The world was filled with places under supernatural protection. Transgressions drew down bad luck, curses, and withdrawal of favor by gods and ancestral ghosts."

"Kate, are you extolling superstition as a restraint on habitat destruction?" demanded Armbruster.

"I'm not saying that superstitions tell truths about animals, rivers, and so on, Armbruster; I'm saying that they tell something true about humankind. And you can't say that fear of retribution is a weak restraint. Right now, in the most scientifically advanced societies, that fear is a potent restraint because, if anything, science has given us scarier reasons than superstition to fear retribution for human damage to the rest of nature. For a very short time, Western civilization minimized this fear in its peoples' mistaken belief that man was divinely installed as lord of nature. But the ancient fear of retribution has returned, and along with it an added terror the ancients didn't confront: Nature and its laws—unlike spirits and gods—are impervious to placating, pleading, and cajoling. Prions and poisons, greenhouse gases and radioactive leaks, oil spills and acid rain—environments damaged by them don't hear our excuses or care about our promises.

"Awe for powers stronger than we are on this earth has also been returning full force. One aspect of awe—the veneration of places because they're holy—has shifted in part to veneration of places because they have significant historic, aesthetic, or ecological value."

"When you first mentioned alternative occupations as restraints," said Hortense, "I thought of how we would look to other animals if they reflected on our behavior the way you reflected on theirs. Surely they'd identify us as creatures devoting remarkable amounts of time, effort, and ingenuity to producing and receiving mouthed noises. The whole human race—from the arctic to the tropics, as you put it—is chattering. The ability to use language is inborn; it enhances our competitive success both as individuals and as a species, and it certainly takes up time, from tribal powwows to chitchat on the Internet. But does it do anything more to restrain habitat destruction than provide alternate harmless occupations?"

"Language isn't harmless," said Kate. "Language infuses everything we think and do, including destroying. But, yes, it also infuses care and respect for environments, both in ancient days and now. Where would either ancient preceptors or modern environmentalists be without the capacity to warn and persuade?"

"I'll put in a vote for our inborn capacity to tinker and contrive," said Hiram. "Sure, like talk, it figures in both habitat destruction and habitat preservation. We have reason to deplore the unintended consequences of fossil fuels, but we should remember that coal mining prevented the complete stripping of forests for fuel and that oil and hydroelectric power, along with the harm done by their unintended consequences, saved us from strip-mining low-grade coal deposits that are viciously polluting. I grant you, the other traits you mention are useful restraints, but they wouldn't get us far if we didn't tinker and contrive.

Time and again, that's what has diverted us from using the same natural resources too monotonously, continually, and ruinously. Woven cloth and rugs were substitutes for animal skins. Columns of quarried stone and walls of brick or adobe were substitutes for timber. Ceramic cutting tools and reinforced plastics are substitutes for metals. If we ever stop tinkering to correct and correct and correct what we do, then we'll bring the world to ruin."

"More likely, bring ourselves to ruin first," said Hortense. "The world's tougher and more resilient than any species, including ours."

"Has anybody another nomination for the traits we're seeking?" asked Kate. "Love of home territory might suggest itself, but it's too self-centered and too little environment-centered. People can be all too willing to victimize other environments if they think that doing so will protect or enhance their own. What's more, taking into account the ground rules—long spans of time, universality, and harmony with competitive success—we must recognize that human beings have not been so tightly attached to home surroundings that they haven't been willing to wander away if alien soil looks more inviting."

She paused and when no one spoke, she continued, "Very well, we have aesthetic appreciation, fear of retribution, awe expressed as veneration, persuasiveness, and corrective tinkering and contriving. These ancient and widespread traits happen to be traits that modern environmental activists display and also depend upon in others. I doubt that this is coincidence. These traits seem to have been components of the human makeup since time immemorial. As Hiram likes to say, they're what we have."

"Kate, you said this has economic relevance," Armbruster said thoughtfully. "Of course I can see the relationship of habitat preservation to economic development, co-development, and diversity, because as Hiram has dinned into us, habitat preservation requires tinkering and contriving—and as he's also dinned into us, successful tinkering and contriving require creative, prospering economies. Also, ecologists, chemists, and biologists—and their cautionary or frightening discoveries—are supported by prosperous economies, not by poor and stagnant economies living hand to mouth.

"But may I make an additional observation about the relevance of the connection between economic life and habitat maintenance? Yes, the habitats in which we're placed include ensembles of the rest of nature; and, yes, it will be as fatal to us as it would be to panthers and elephants were we to destroy our natural habitat irretrievably; and, yes, I'm willing to suppose that evolution has provided us with restraining traits that may just possibly prevent us from destroying the rest of the natural world.

"But as human beings, our habitats also consist of our own settlements and the economic ensembles on which they depend. It's no accident that we find the most successful economic enterprises within the most successful economies—not in impoverished economies dominated, say, by all-powerful landlords who end up poor themselves—great at winning the prize as top dogs but rotten at preserving economic habitat.

"I'm not sanguine about evolution having equipped us with inborn traits for preserving economic habitats that—at least in terms of commerce—may be only ten thousand or at most some twenty thousand years old. As a species, we're susceptible to white-collar crime, organized crime, freelance crime, ruthless and exploitative governments, and megalomaniacs, all of which are ready, willing, and able to kill the geese that lay the golden eggs to satisfy their own lust for power, fortunes, or vainglory or to impose their own visions of utopia, no matter what economic harm it does to the arenas in which they compete. The horrors of which they're capable could be expanded indefinitely: deadly weapons, germ warfare, genocide, ethnic cleansing, and campaigns to mobilize popular hysterias and hatreds that make the other horrors practically possible. What protection did evolution give us against this?"

"Not much, I'm afraid," Hiram replied as Kate hesitated and looked taken aback. "Only intelligence. No, wait a minute. Perhaps I'm wrong. We have some sense of morality—another gift of consciousness. Definitions of right and wrong don't cut across the board, but consciousness of right and wrong behavior is a very ancient and widespread trait. You know that yourselves, Armbruster, Kate, and Hortense. I read your book on the symbiosis between government and economic life, which at bottom deals with the subject you've just brought up. You're right that failure to respect that symbiosis and the morals upholding it dead-ends prospering economic life.

"But I'll add one more sin to the list that Armbruster has mentioned: ignorance, for which the remedies are awareness and knowledge. Why do you think I—"

The door of the dining room opened, and Murray poked in his head. "I must have dozed off," he said. "The garden's dried off enough. Come on outside."

"Can't; there's the recorder," said Armbruster.

"I've already rigged up an extension cord from the basement. Let's go. It's too beautiful outside to hang around indoors."

Chapter 7

UNPREDICTABILITY

Hiram's garden boasted two handsome sycamores, a thicket of lilac bushes, and a bed of English ivy on which a fox's head and foreleg were emerging from a block of red sandstone. "Young Joel's work, from when he was planning to be a sculptor," said Murray to Kate as they accepted gin and tonics from Hortense and made their way to a cluster of olive-green lawn chairs.

Armbruster, who had worried that extraneous noises would muffle the clarity of voices on tape, was gratified with the garden's serenity and quiet. Houses on Hiram's street shared common side walls, an arrangement that buffered their rear from street sounds. Musing on his good fortune that, owing to damp grass, neighbors were not using lawn mowers, he briefly mistook Hiram's opening remark about "the butterfly effect" for an ecological comment on the garden's insect life.

He was quickly put on track by Hortense. "It's so far-fetched—the idea that a butterfly beating its wings in a

Colorado meadow can lead to a storm and flood three thousand miles away. I'm surprised it's taken so seriously."

"The story behind the butterfly effect has profoundly revised ideas about predictable outcomes," said Hiram. "Classic experimental science for the past three centuries concentrated on discovering cause-and-effect relationships by excluding all but two, or at most three, variables. For instance, rats given diets lacking vitamin A could be compared with a group of rats exactly the same in all respects except that vitamin A was included in their diet. Any differences that emerged between the two groups could reasonably be attributed to effects of the vitamin. Furthermore, any laboratories repeating the experiment with the same care could be expected to get the same results; if they didn't, the validity of the first experiment was called into doubt. 'Can it be replicated?' was the first question demanded of an experiment. Cause-and-effect experiments of this type not only inform; they predict. The key to their success is reduction of the number of variables being investigated.

"In contrast, a cause-and-effect exploration that incorporates even four or five interacting variables is formidably complex. The difficulty is that any one variable may affect one or more of the other variables, which may then affect the others, including the variable at the start of the process, bewilderingly tangling causes and effects into complex webs. Such problems, not being linear and simple, are not susceptible to reductive experiments; the content can't usefully be separated into artificial fragments. This is the sort of problem, for instance, that can arise when scientists turn from *What* does vitamin A do? to *How* does it do what it does?

"Scientists have commonly supposed, or at least hoped,

that if only all the different interacting variables in a web-like relationship could actually be tracked, then multivariable interactions would be predictable, as well as more understandable. Computers hold out that promise because they can handle complexities which are impractical to analyze otherwise on account of the number of calculations and comparisons involved."

"Aha, a bifurcation in analytical techniques was needed," said Armbruster.

"For some complex problems, computers have fulfilled that expectation," Hiram continued, "but not all. Here's where we come to the butterfly beating its wings and generating a zephyr. In 1963, Edward Lorenz, a mathematician and meteorologist, hoped to demonstrate a method for making reliable long-range weather predictions. He entered into a computer an archive of weather-system patterns, complete with their measurable variables, such as temperatures, barometric pressures, wind directions and speeds, precipitation, and influence of adjoining weather fronts. Each pattern's characteristics were stored in the computer's memory. His idea was that a meteorologist could feed into a computer a current weather pattern and instruct the machine to find an exact match in its memory archive. Logically, the subsequent behavior of the past pattern should forecast the subsequent behavior of the matching pattern.

"He set about testing the method by requesting the computer to find matching patterns already in its archives, which it did. Then he examined whether subsequent behavior of those patterns continued to match. A huge surprise awaited him. After only a few days as a rule, and at most a week, matching weather patterns did not continue behaving alike; their subsequent behavior was as dissimilar to each other's as it was to behavior of unmatched patterns. Lorenz says he realized then that reliably predicting weather for more than a week in advance was inherently impossible, but he also realized that he had unpredictably hit upon a discovery with wider and very important implications.

"The weather behaved unpredictably for interesting reasons. The immediate cause must be that obscure, unforeseeable, and idiosyncratic events were producing disproportionately large consequences, hence the shorthand expression *the butterfly effect.*"

"The triviality of it—that's what's so far-fetched," said Hortense.

"Not really," said Kate. "The idea is that small events produce disproportionately large consequences owing to changes that become exaggerated as they reverberate among variables. We know that this happens. The amount of freon released by aerosol cans and discarded refrigerators containing the gas is a pittance in the great oceans of air. Yet because of the reaction of that pittance with ozone, freon causes holes in the canopy that shields earth from the full force of ultraviolet rays. Or think, Hortense, how a tiny, obscure encounter between an invading virus and one of your patrolling immune cells can set in motion a web of events within your body that determine whether you live or die."

"The symbolic butterfly doesn't mean merely that small causes can have disproportionately large consequences," said Hiram. "That's long been observed. As the old saying has it, the kingdom was lost for want of a horseshoe nail. Nor is the meaning of the butterfly merely that it can be impossible to take into account every cause, influence, and interrelationship in a complex system, owing to causes being too many, subtle, varied, and volatile.

"The major jolt packed into Lorenz's discovery was this: Even if every single influence on some types of complex systems could be accurately taken into account, their futures would still be unpredictable."

"Why do you say that?" asked Hortense. "How can you know that?"

"A system can be making itself up as it goes along," said Hiram. "The weather is like that. Evolution is like that. Economies, if they aren't inert and stagnant, are like that. Since they make themselves up as they proceed, they aren't predestined. Not being predestined, they aren't predictable."

"That may be a novel idea for meteorologists, but it's old news to linguists," said Armbruster. "Speakers make a language and yet nobody, including its speakers or scholars, can predict its future vocabulary or usages, precisely for the reason you've said: Language makes itself up as it goes along. Even when languages start out the same, like those weather patterns, they diverge idiosyncratically. Who could have predicted French, Spanish, Portuguese, Mallorcan, Provençal, Romanian, or even Florentine Italian and Sicilian Italian from Latin? Who could have forecast the English we're speaking now by analyzing the English in *Beowulf*, or even *The Canterbury Tales*? Who can predict English vocabulary and usages in the year 2800? Or the differences it will display then in different places where it's spoken? Of course," he added reflectively, "languages do have rules of grammar, fairly consistent ways of adapting what they borrow from other languages, and even somewhat reliable patterns of pronunciation shifts."

"Yes, languages aren't gibberish," said Hiram. "Creative self-organization—which is what we're talking about—doesn't imply disorder. On the contrary. But it tells us that order is not uniformity, and that what is created within a framework of orderly processes is not predestined or predictable.

"In an ecosystem," he went on, "plants and animals pursue what amount to plans for the future. They do this even though they lack consciousness of the future, at least in the same sense we're aware of it. They construct nests, dig burrows, establish families, locate food sources, put down roots, germinate fruits. Together they compose an ecosystem, much as collections of enterprises with their plans for the future compose a settlement's economy. The ecosystem doesn't and can't impose hierarchical command over the ensemble, which is self-organized and is making itself up as it goes along."

"That's beautifully elucidated in *The Beak of the Finch*, another book I reviewed," said Kate.

"Nobody commands an economy that has vitality and potential," said Hiram. "It springs surprise upon surprise instead of knuckling down and doing what's expected of it, or wished for it."

"But surely if you had it in your power, Hiram, you'd get the government to mandate reforms eliminating vicious circles and tell enterprises what they must do with respect to pollution, waste of resources, and so on," said Armbruster.

"It's not in my power, but more to the point, it isn't in the power of governments to do that successfully, either—not in the sense of laying out just what is to be done. I don't know what's to be done or what's possible to do, and neither does anyone else, whether in government or out. Like my clients searching for ways to make materials at life-friendly temperatures and for materials and their products that will be benignly biodegradable when users are finished with them, some members of the ensemble may come up with what's needed, but they must depend on the rest of the ensemble—on the co-developments of other members, and on many, many others in the ensemble, to keep the whole precarious contraption stable enough and expanding enough to assimilate corrections and bifurcations."

"Hubris—overweening confidence," said Murray. "Economic history is stuffed with expensive duds undertaken by people who thought they could predict the future by shaping it. The foreign-aid import-substitution fiasco is an example: big, quick fixes for big problems. We have our own examples. By hindsight, it's apparent that nuclear power isn't the cheap and harmless energy it was expected to be. In addition to radioactivity's hazards for people who deal with it, radioactive wastes are so dangerous, far into the future."

"But nuclear power sounded promising for reducing atmospheric pollution and acid rain," Armbruster protested. "How can economies find out what's workable without trying? Hiram, you yourself favor experimenting. Shouldn't we at least try to plan corrections when it's plain that only a significant new fork in the road will answer? And push as hard as possible when we recognize that we need the new fork quickly?"

"The mistake is to conclude in advance that you already have the answer you need," said Hiram. "Maybe you do, but probably you don't. Successful bifurcations tend to start modestly and be tested out as they work their way into economic life—or else are dropped. While hundreds of billions of dollars were being force-fed into nuclear power, other possibilities were being starved, neglected, and derided. That's not an experimental approach."

"Hindsight is notoriously clear and foresight notoriously fallible," said Kate. " 'Fulton's Folly' was the popular epithet for the first American steamboat. Cries of 'Get a horse!' greeted early automobile users. The leading early computer manufacturer, IBM, was convinced that computers would remain too expensive and cumbersome for individual ownership."

"Experts on industrial materials dismissed plastics as useful only for kitchen gadgets and toys," said Murray.

"Who in the world thought that?" asked Hortense.

"For one, the technical editor of what at the time—this was in the early 1940s—was the leading U.S. trade journal for the metal industries."

"It's still common to dismiss ecologists and environmental activists as cranks, and organic farmers and proponents of solar energy as hobbyists," said Kate. "At least wind-generated energy and material recycling are being taken seriously and finding economic niches. Does initial skepticism matter?"

"It matters," Murray put in, "when potential bifurcations can't get capital or necessary permissions or are not allowed to break into monopolized fields."

"To be sure, it's possible for society to set goals, and in some cases even standards, for results wanted," said Hiram. "And, of course, it's possible to forbid arrantly destructive environmental behavior—in the same way as we forbid arrantly destructive behavior to one another, such as looting, cheating, and defrauding. But mandating environmental goals or standards doesn't mean mandating how they're to be reached.

"Nobody can predict better ways, let alone 'best' ways, of doing familiar things—to say nothing of things not previously done at all. Ancient as the problem of sewage-contaminated water is, and ancient as some of its solutions are, we're still discovering new and better ways of addressing this environmental and economic problem. It's fine for governments to mandate permissible bacterial counts and parts per million of other contaminants, but the worst thing governments could do would be to mandate how standards are to be achieved. As I mentioned when discussing development and co-development, that would freeze development at its current and still unsatisfactory stage."

"Everybody talks about how amazing it is that the Internet is self-organized," said Hortense. "Also, how remarkable that a system which originated when a very few computer users in universities and government offices, who had common research interests, linked their computers by telephone lines—how remarkable that it's ramified itself into a 'World Wide Web' by making itself up as it went along. Nobody planned such a thing. Is the Internet unusual?"

"It's unusual in having grown so big so rapidly," Murray answered. "Notice the expression *World Wide Web* that you just used. Everybody understands the Internet as a web. As for its being self-organized, that isn't novel. We look at established ways of doing things, formalized in large and well-established organizations, and tend thoughtlessly to suppose they were born so. Take civilian postal systems, now largely superseded by E-mail, faxes, and courier services. It used to be that a person in Europe or America with a letter or parcel to send outside the locality entrusted it to someone going that way—a ship's officer, say, or a coachman, a merchant, or somebody in a merchant's entourage. Customarily, the recipient of the letter or parcel, not the sender, paid the carrier. That was a precaution against the carrier agreeing to make the delivery but neglecting or being unable to do so. A self-organizing postal system can be said to have started when senders took letters to coaching inns or waterfront taverns and travelers hoping to pick up side money took to dropping by these posts and picking up letters awaiting carriage. Senders, carriers, and inn proprietors were creating proto–postal systems, mail depots linked together—a primitive Internet. When governments formalized the service in the nineteenth century, they monopolized it and incorporated improvements, among them payment by the sender, not the recipient. That change protected the postal systems' interests, and it was practical because governments guaranteed reliable delivery by enforcing honest and diligent behavior on carriers. But for all their power, governments eventually couldn't maintain their monopolies, although they tried. Independent courier services began illegally; they flourished because they occupied niches that the postal services weren't filling satisfactorily.

"Credit cards; equipment leasing; franchising; organic farming and marketing nowadays—and farming at all in the first place—don't be misled by their established appearances into thinking that they started out as they are today or that they were expected at the time they emerged.

"In 1992, on a visit to Hong Kong," Murray went on, "I saw a small yet global self-organized market in action. I was strolling and gawking along a street on the fringe of a vast outdoor jade-jewelry market—which, incidentally, had been self-organized by stall proprietors and had burgeoned to unanticipated size—when I noticed a knot of a dozen or so young men showing each other envelopes of rock fragments and jotting down notations, using the top of a parked car as their desk. I was told they were jade traders and that the notations they were making would set world prices of jade for that day. It recalled to my mind that the New York Stock Exchange was started on a Wall Street sidewalk under a buttonwood tree. That's an old-fashioned name for a sycamore or plane tree, like those two that Hiram has."

"I like that about the parked car used as a desk," said Kate. "A desk is an extension of a lap. Technologies are extensions of our bodies: microscopes and telescopes, extensions of eyes; telephone receivers, extensions of ears; pens, extensions of fingers, and writing, extensions of voices; wheels, extensions of leg and back muscles; spears, extensions of arms. Weapons are still called arms."

"The bones inside an arm—you may not know this—" said Hiram, "are waste. Or were, to begin with. Excess calcium within cells is poisonous; they rid themselves of it. In the course of evolution, that particular discard found use as shells, skeletons, and teeth. Useful recycling of discards is an ancient stratagem of life. Of course human beings have long used that same stratagem consciously, but still not as marvelously as our own cells use it."

"Our seamless, total connectedness within nature— that's what Ben wouldn't hear of or think of in his contempt for what he called unnatural," said Kate.

"It would have interfered with his enjoyment of hating technology and business," said Armbruster. "Balderdash!"

"Of course the idea that we, and what we do, aren't natural is balderdash," said Hiram. "If our doings aren't natural, then by definition they must be supernatural. Spears, cars, and computers aren't supernatural. To get back to my own obsession, economies aren't supernatural, either, although economists act as if they are when they ignore such realities as that economies require diversity to expand, self-refueling to maintain themselves, and co-developments to develop. No wonder well-intentioned people like Ben pick up the absurd notion that economic life is arbitrary and un-natural."

"Wait a minute," said Hortense. "Balderdash that may be, but balderdash is natural, too. Evolution provided us with consciousness, right? Because we have consciousness, we also have the ability to make mistakes. We make more mistakes—or, anyhow, different mistakes—than other animals can make. For us that's natural, isn't it?"

"Yes it is," said Murray, "but consciousness also gives us the ability to recognize mistakes."

"The saving grace that accompanies the hazard," said Armbruster. "But let's not get into a discussion of free will. Everything that can be said on that subject has already been said."

"Don't be too sure about that," said Hiram. "Consciousness itself is still a mystery. How can the mind observe itself as if it existed outside itself? It's the ability to separate ourselves from ourselves inwardly which leads to the conceit that we're above nature or, as Ben sees it, in an adversarial position."

"If and when neurophysiologists find out how a brain manages to be conscious of itself as a willful, judgmental 'me,' what they'll tell us will be about proteins, enzymes, cilia, and electrical nerve impulses," said Hortense. "It will be boring and incomprehensible to most of us."

"But it will be even more remarkable than we can imagine," said Hiram. "The more we know of nature's operations, the more wondrous nature is seen to be. And when and if we get a real science of economics—"

"And where will that come from?" asked Hortense.

"I don't know," said Hiram. "It doesn't look all that

promising. Maybe from a symbiosis of nonsupernatural economics with nonmisanthropic ecology. We need it. So far, our horrible mistakes notwithstanding, we're still accepted within the great ensemble of species. So we still have opportunities to establish ourselves in the ensemble a bit more securely as symbionts than we're warranted to suppose we are now. Whether or not we'll muff it isn't predictable, because we'll be making ourselves up as we go along—just as we've always done so far.

"In spite of my panegyrics to nature's order," Hiram went on, "nature is far from perfect by criteria that would guide what we conceive of as intelligent, careful planning. Embryos go awry in their development. Species fail to adjust to changed circumstances and go extinct. A case can be made that development and co-development foster disorder by throwing new uncertainties into the pot. But within the confusion, redundancy, and unpredictability, the stupendous processes we've been discussing are operating: development and co-development through differentiation; expansion through diversification; continuation through self-refueling; stabilization through self-correction—all brought into order through unpredictable self-organization."

Murray raised his glass. "To the unpredictable, uncommandable future in the making. And to not forgetting that 'in the making' is always and forever *now*. And now I must leave. A farmer friend of mine wants a hive of bees, and I think one of mine is preparing to swarm. His daughter's at my place keeping watch, but she's a novice at handling them. The sooner they swarm the better, with June almost half gone already. An old jingle claims that a swarm in May is worth a load of hay, a swarm in June is worth a silver spoon, and a swarm in July is not worth a fly."

"Why is that?" asked Hortense.

"A swarm in July barely has time to lay up its food for the winter—none left over for the beekeeper. There's a principle you can count on, no matter what happens to the comparative prices of hay, silver, and honey."

"Before you go, one more question," said Hortense. "What are economies *for?* Of course I know they're to supply human needs, but surely human needs include fair and just sharing of economic production."

"You put me in mind of how my grandfather thought about nature," said Murray. "What is nature *for?* He'd have said, 'It's to supply the needs of mankind.' Being a pious man, he'd have added, 'So that mankind may bear witness to the abounding mercy of God.' Being a lawyer and humanist, you say, 'So that people may evince justice and fairness to one another.' Tell me, Hortense, would you give the same answer as my grandfather to the question of what nature is for?"

"No, of course not. Nature has value and integrity in its own right, regardless of human needs. I see what you're driving at. You think my idea of what economies are for is equally superficial. But people don't create or possess nature, and they do create and possess economies."

Hiram sighed and reentered the conversation. "To be sure, people create and possess things that they cast up by grace of the processes of economic life. But our naked, unlettered ancestors didn't create those processes of development and diversification and neither did we. This much I know: It's stupid to try to circumvent universal processes. I don't know what economies are for, ultimately, other than to enable us to partake, in our own fashion, in a great universal flow. What do the rest of you think?"

"I think economic life is for teaching our species it has responsibilities to the planet and the rest of nature," said Kate. "At least that's my hope. In its own way, that isn't so far from bearing witness, Murray. It isn't so far, either, from Hortense's aim for justice and fairness, although I'm including other forms of life besides ours."

"I have two thoughts on the question," said Armbruster. "First, beware of drift into ideology. Economic ideologies are a curse. Carts before horses, tails wagging dogs, self-imposed blinders! I prefer Murray's dry proposal to look factually into import-stretching ratios, skeptical though I was when he suggested it."

"I think they'd give us some large surprises," said Murray.

"Second," Armbruster went on, "it seems to me that economies have a lot in common with language—a lot besides unpredictably making themselves up. What is language for? The glib answer is communication, which you could say of the yips of coyotes and pheromones of termites. Not an answer that does justice to the functions of language. How about this? Language is also for learning and to pass along learning, in the process permitting us to develop cultures and multitudes of purposes. Just so, economies are to fill material needs, which you could also say of the foraging of deer and the scavenging of buzzards. Not an answer that does justice to the functions of economies. Like language, economic life permits us to develop cultures and multitudes of purposes, and in my opinion, that's its function which is most meaningful for us."

"I'll go along with that," said Murray. "Now, I really must leave and pay attention to those bees."

Chapter 8

ARMBRUSTER'S PROMISE

On a Monday morning a month later, Armbruster was reading the newspaper in his restaurant hangout when Kate dropped by. "Hear anything lately about Hortense and Hiram?" she asked.

"Not a word. Say, here's an item which says that about seven days' worth of hair clippings from the two hundred thousand U.S. hair salons, done up in mesh pillows, could have completely soaked up the Valdez oil spill in about one week. In contrast, Exxon spent two billion dollars on a lengthy cleanup that captured only twelve percent of the spill. The hair method has been discovered by an Alabama hairdresser, who saw a photograph of an oil-soaked Valdez otter, thought about its oil-saturated fur, and began experimenting with bundles of hair clippings and motor oil in his toddler's wading pool. A customer put him in touch with a 'technology transfer expert,' who arranged successful laboratory tests. Hair picks up and holds oil because——"

Someone sat down in the booth, next to Kate. She and

Armbruster both looked up, startled. "Murray!" said Kate. "I was just wondering—"

"I've only got a minute," said Murray, who looked tired and haggard. "I have a cab waiting outside. Hortense said I'd find you here. Armbruster, I want to ask a favor. Hiram's so wrapped up in other projects I doubt he'll ever get back to economics. A shame. His ideas might be useful. Don't pressure him—but if he agrees, would you see that his ideas get into publishable form and are published? I know that's a lot to ask." He stood up. "Now I have to be off."

"Where?" asked Armbruster.

"The hospital. They've scheduled an operation for me tomorrow, and I'm due to check in for more tests and stuff"—he looked at his wristwatch—"five minutes ago."

"Where's Hiram?" asked Kate.

"He and Hortense will come by this afternoon to see that I'm properly looked after."

"If Hiram wants me to do that, yes I will, Murray. You can depend on it," said Armbruster, extending his hand to shake. "Shall I go over to the hospital with you?"

"No, but thanks. Everything's arranged."

When Kate and Armbruster returned to their coffee after seeing Murray into his cab, Armbruster said, "I knew from the minute Hiram opened his mouth that making those tapes was a good idea. If he agrees that I can work them up, do you want to help?"

"You edit the transcripts, and I'll put in the descriptive bits," said Kate. "What will you call it?"

"How about *The Ecology of Human Beings?*"

"Ummm. No. The ecology of human beings . . . the ecology of black bears . . . the ecology of morning glories. . . . It misses the point of ecology. You can't isolate one species and refer to ecology. Remember, Hiram's point is that human beings aren't in isolation from the rest of nature. How about *An Economic Primer?* He deals with basics that orthodox economic texts don't go into."

"Hummm. No. Anybody seeing that title on the jacket would expect a baby-talk introduction to orthodox economics. Or maybe simple advice on managing their money. How about *Human Beings in the Ecology?*"

"Ummm. I like it better than your first suggestion, but it's too broad. After all, this is specifically about economics."

"Well, the title can wait. Maybe something in the transcript will jump out. Of course, Hiram might balk at the whole idea. I hope not. As Murray said, it might be useful."

Epilogue

Hiram was delighted to have Armbruster relieve him of the book. Murray recovered from surgery well enough to attend and enjoy Hiram and Hortense's wedding in the fall. Murray was also able to read, correct, and approve a draft of Armbruster's edited transcript, which was little different from the published version. Hiram supplied the title. Kate and Hortense agreed that Armbruster looked five years younger after he went to work on the book. He gave up hanging out in the restaurant and never noticed when it went out of business, replaced by a florist.

Notes

Note sequences follow chapter texts.

1. Damn, Another Ecologist

Biomimicry is by Janine M. Benyus (New York: Morrow, 1997). *Eco-Pioneers*, by Steve Lerner (Cambridge, Mass.: MIT, 1997), describes innovative products and practices learned from nature that are constructive and ingenious but less ambitious and complicated than those dealt with in *Biomimicry*. Other ventures into biomimicry are described in *Restoring the Earth: Visionary Solutions from the Bioneers*, by Kenny Ausubel (Tiburon, Calif.: Kramer, 1997). *Collective Heritage*, newsletter of the Bioneer movement (Santa Fe, N.M.), carries ongoing news of successful or promising biomimicry; for example, its spring 1998 issue contains information on phytomediation, use of plants that accumulate metals, to decontaminate polluted soil; and on an outstandingly successful Virginia farm, whose owners have modeled symbiotic cattle, chicken, and egg farming on the prairie relationship of bison and prairie chickens. "Human Domination of Earth's Ecosystems," by Peter M. Vitousek, et al., in *Science* (July 25, 1997), discusses, among other things, interventions to hasten restoration of abused ecosystems and points out that these are most successful if they "use or mimic natural processes."

The *Oxford English Dictionary*, defining *ecology*, under its initial spelling, *oecology*, as "the science of the economy of animals and plants," dates the word's first written appearance in English to 1873 and notes that the coinage follows *economy*. Initially, *oecology* referred to both animal and plant communities, but under its modern spelling, dated as 1896, the word denoted only plant communities until 1930, when animals were again included.

Industrial uses of bacteria are constantly being discovered or rediscovered—e.g., Philip John, a plant biochemist at the University of Reading, England, has discovered that a bacterium called *Clostridium* is responsible for converting leaves of the woad plant into indigo. The process, which John reconstructed from a manual compiled by early American colonists, is potentially important both economically and ecologically, to reduce the pollution that results from dyeing blue denim.

The hormone-mimicking chemical pollutants to which Hortense refers are discussed in *Our Stolen Future,* by Colborn, Dumanoski, and Myers (New York: Dutton, 1996).

2. THE NATURE OF DEVELOPMENT

Ontogeny and Phylogeny, by Stephen Jay Gould (Cambridge, Mass.: Belknap/Harvard, 1977), a technical text on evolutionary development, also traces the history of the understanding of development as a process, which transformed the term *evolution* from preformation to its modern sense of organic change (p. 28 ff.) K. E. von Baer (1792–1876), a German embryologist who was an intellectual pioneer in several other scientific fields as well, stated as a law of embryonic development: "Less general characters are developed from the most general, and so forth, until finally the most specialized appear." Moreover, as Gould points out, von Baer recognized that he had identified a general or universal law of development: "It is the same thought that, in the cosmos, collects the separated masses into spheres and binds these together into a solar system; the same that allows the scattered dust on the surface of the metallic planet to develop into living forms . . ." His insight was paraphrased by evolutionists, sometimes as "heterogeneity emerging from homogeneity" (p. 52 ff. and p. 109 ff.). The wording in the paraphrase I have employed is conventional today.

Symbiotic Planet: A New View of Evolution, by Lynn Margulis (New York: Basic Books, 1998), is a good introduction to bacterial and single-cell life forms and the symbiotic origins of our own cells' organelles. As she points out, symbiosis not only involves two (or sometimes more) types of organisms that benefit from mutual support but in effect creates another organism which can do or be things the symbionts cannot do or be except in combination. *Lives of a Cell,* by Lewis Thomas (New York: Viking, 1974), includes, along with much else worth reading, a charmingly written and scientifically accurate essay on mitochondria. A good account of chloroplasts and their work of photosynthesis as symbionts in green plants is included in *Biomimicry* (n. Ch. 1).

The honey bird and its ways were described in Botswana by local people to Alana Probst, who passed their information along to me. The skunklike mammal is a ratel, native to Africa and India. The honey bird, under the name "honey guide," is defined in the *Random House Dictionary* as native to Africa and southern Asia, "certain species of which are noted for their habit of leading men or animals to nests of honeybees . . ." According to Probst's informants in Botswana, if a hunter is so foolish as to not share the hive with the bird, he will never again be led to a hive, but she was informed that this cannot be verified, "because nobody is that foolish."

Helena Cronin points out in *The Ant and the Peacock* (Cambridge: Cambridge University Press, 1991) that the description of nature as "red in tooth and claw" is pre-Darwinian, having been published in 1850 in a poem by Tennyson. It "reflected a view of nature that was common both inside and outside science at that time. . . . Darwin and Wallace, no less than their contemporaries, were heirs to this bleak tradition" (p. 273).

Muscle was cited as a fractal by Janine Benyus (Biomimicry's author) in reply to a question from the audience at a lecture in October 1997 in Toronto. Color illustrations (these things need to be in color) of computer-generated fractals accompany "Computer Recreations," by A. K. Dewdney, *Scientific American* (August 1985).

The *Titanic's* steel was analyzed in the materials laboratory of the Canadian Dept. of National Defense, Halifax, using plates recovered from the wreck; "The Other Lessons from the *Titanic,*" by John MacIntyre, *The Globe and Mail* (Toronto, April 18, 1998).

Differentiations emerging from generalities are exhibited by bodies of knowledge unless and until they become fossilized. E.g., from the generality of history (what happened?) have emerged archaeology, archives, biography, historical novels and dramas, memoirs, prehistoric-dating technology, histories of science, medicine, art, civil rights, and industries, women's studies, etc. The many life sciences, as well as seismology, plate tectonics, mineral and oil exploration, etc., have emerged from the generality once known as natural philosophy.

Discoveries of previously unseen co-development and interdependencies, both historical and current, come thick and fast nowadays. A couple of examples: Archaeologists have learned, to their surprise, that in the second millennium B.C., Mesopotamians manufactured synthetic stone for construction and for grinding grain by melting basalt silt, then slowly cooling it—a sophisticated technology that must have required potters and smiths to pool their skills and knowledge; *Science News* (vol. 153, p. 407). Experiments in a British Columbia forest reveal that birches subsidize firs with carbon in the form of a sugar transported by underground fungi networks embracing roots of both tree species. When researchers shaded firs with heavy cloth canopies, birches and fungi increased the quantities of carbon supplied them. The finding contradicts ecosystem models which assume that plants constantly compete for resources, and also suggests how some plants growing in shade during long periods of their early life may receive nourishment in spite of being light-starved; *Science News* (vol. 152, p. 87).

The relationship between "giving" and "trading" in Old English is explained in *Our Marvelous Native Tongue*, by Robert Claiborne (New York: Times Books, 1983), p. 80.

The new practices of commercial recyclers and charities that collect old clothes are described in "Squeeze Is on Charities as Cheap Becomes Chic" [a wildly misleading headline], by Ljeoma Ross, *The Globe and Mail* (Toronto, November 2, 1996). A typical flier, headed "Save Time and Frustration" and "Your Waste Is Someone Else's Need," specifies items wanted, pickup day, means of identifying a bag for the collector by attaching a flier; it also requests donors to call police or the company if rival recyclers are seen hijacking donations. Having used the system as operated by both a charity and a commercial recycler, I can attest to its efficiency.

The fifteenth-century copper-wire process used by IBM chip engineers was reported in *The Economist*, reprinted in *The Globe and Mail* (Toronto, July 11, 1998).

Kate's supposition about disappearance of new manual typewriters is premature: e.g., a Hammacher Schlemmer mail order catalogue (New York, 1999) advertises portable manual Olivetti typewriters. Vanished repair mechanics are a different matter.

The number of people employed in the Soviet Union's economic planning bureaucracy is routinely reported in the North American press to have been 8 million.

For information on Turkish rug dyes and the rejuvenation of splendid weaving, I am indebted to Max Allen, a founder of the Textile Museum in Toronto. He is also a radio producer for the Canadian Broadcasting Corporation and the source of my information on the swift obsolescence of recording technology. The machine that couldn't be found to play back interviews was Memocord, a highly successful Viennese technology in its day.

The Clock of the Long Now, by Stewart Brand (New York: Basic Books, 1999), discusses total loss of content on quickly decaying computer discs and tapes, along with possible strategies for transferring content; pp. 82–92.

3. THE NATURE OF EXPANSION

The farm with the early generator and prize butter is modeled on a general and dairy farm in Delaware County, New York, whose owner was a friend of the older generation of my husband's family. The engineer's career is modeled on my father-in-law's. The career of "Joel and Jenny" is modeled on that of a couple who told me their story in 1937 in what is now SoHo, New York City.

Discoveries of single-cell organisms in unlikely places and estimates of volume of underground bacterial life are summarized by Ricardo Guerrero and Lynn Margulis in *The Sciences* (New York Academy of Sciences, July/August, 1998).

Tropical Nature, by Adrian Forsyth and Ken Miyata (New York: Macmillan, 1984), describes the meager productivity, and reasons for it, of tropical-rain-forest soils after forests have been cleared for farming. The close relationship between volume of biomass and number of species was measured by a research team from the universities of Minnesota and Toronto, who planted and tended 147 plots of Minnesota prairie, each plot planted with one to twenty-four native species singly and in various combinations. The outcome showed that the greater the number of species in a plot, the larger the volume of biomass produced; also, the greater the number of species, the more nitrogen they extracted from the soil, while the fewer the species, the more nitrogen leached out of the soil, unused. The researchers concluded that Darwin was correct when he suggested that the more species on a piece of land, the more efficient was the use of its resources—but they added that they did not understand the mechanics at work; *The Globe and Mail* (Toronto, March 9, 1996). A similar relationship was reported by William F. Laurance and Thomas E. Lovejoy in *Science* (November 7, 1997). They studied remnant pockets of forest in Brazil ten to seventeen years after areas surrounding the pockets had been logged. The remnant pockets contained fewer plant and animal species than plots of the same size within intact forests. The remnants also contained less volume of biomass (the research teams measured the diameter of 56,000 trees). In some cases, the decline in diversity was accompanied by as much as a 36 percent decline in biomass.

Possibly because so many ambitious and expensive attempts to force or coax economic expansion have failed during the second half of the twentieth century, it has finally become permissible to say that the emperor has no clothes—that economic theory can't explain economic expansion. For example, a roundup article, "The Chemistry of Growth," in *The Economist* (March 5, 1999), begins: "Economic growth is notoriously the blackest of the many black boxes in economics," and after breezily disposing of current explanations, it concludes: "What is the main thing governments must do to spur economic growth? Ah, well, that remains a mystery." I would add that *The Economist*'s question is the wrong way to approach the mystery, which is essentially a question of what *economies* do.

Anomalies of city economic expansion in some cases, the sporadicity of expansion in all cases, and reasons for these peculiarities are discussed in the chapter "Explosive City Growth" in my book *The Economy of Cities* (New York: Random House, 1969, and Vintage, 1970).

Sally Goerner, author of *Chaos and the Evolving Ecological Universe* (Langhorne, Pa.: Gordon and Breach, 1994), points out that although discharged energy is lost at the macro-scale of machines, "this doesn't necessarily mean the energy is 'lost' as used to be assumed. The 'lost energy' engages in a different form of work; e.g., heat lost by an engine, thereby lost to the work being done by the engine, does work at the atomic scale. What was lost at the macro-scale is alive and well at the micro-scale" (personal communication).

Ecotrust, an organization devoted to conservation-based development in coastal temperate rain forests of Pacific North America, aptly calls resources such as forests, water, and fish "natural capital." If renewable resources are prudently stretched by being combined with human capital and effort, only the yield from natural capital is extracted, not the capital itself; *Natural Capital in the Rain Forests of Home,* by Spencer B. Beebe (Portland, Ore.: Ecotrust, 1998).

The microchip is cited as an example of import stretching (although he doesn't call it that) by Tachi Kiuchi, chairman and CEO of Mitsubishi Electric America. "A microchip's physical content isn't very valuable. Silica is the cheapest and most abundant raw material on the planet—sand. But a microchip—its shape, its design, its unseen artistry—is extremely valuable. Yet it comes from a source that seems almost unlimited—the knowledge and inspiration that we draw from the human mind and spirit. This is the most valuable resource and the most abundant"; speech to business executives in Washington, D.C., June 1997. Kiuchi is a leader in an association of corporations emphasizing the desirability of shifting investments away from ecologically harmful products and practices and taking corporate responsibility for the ecological impact of products "from cradle to cradle," meaning from design through manufacturing and use to eventual reuse or recycling as manufactured products or compost. An architect who teaches this approach to architectural and product design students, and also uses it in his own architecture and design practice, is William McDonough, of Charlottesville, Virginia. Readers of Paul Hawken's books are also familiar with these ideas.

Robert Lucas, professor of economics at the University of Chicago and winner of the 1995 Nobel Prize in economics, identified human capital as a major economic resource, introduced it into economic models, and pointed out that this resource does not become exhausted by use; "On the Mechanics of Economic Development," *Journal of Monetary Economics* (22: 3–42, 1988). A student of Lucas, Paul Romer, now professor of economics at Stanford University, has pursued this line of thought with emphasis on the role of human capital in technological change; "Increasing Returns and Long-Run Growth," *Journal of Political Economy* (94: 1002–1037, 1986). The reception of Romer's ideas by economists (some welcome them; some do not) is reviewed by Bernard Wysocki, Jr., in *The Wall Street Journal*, reprinted in *The Globe and Mail* (Toronto, February 15, 1997).

4. THE NATURE OF SELF-REFUELING

Gaia: A New Look at Life on Earth, by James Lovelock, was first published in 1979 (Oxford: Oxford University Press) and reissued by the same publisher in a revised and corrected edition in 1995. *The Ages of Gaia: A Biography of Our Living Earth,* by Lovelock (New York: Norton, 1988), technically describes chemical composition and evolution of the biosphere. Lovelock's hypothesis of earth as a self-evolving, self-regulating entity was originally scorned by most other scientists, as were earlier versions of the same concept of earth that had been proposed during the past century. But the hypothesis has now been upgraded to theory by scientists generally and has been given the name "earth system science." History of the idea, before and since Lovelock's works, is briefly surveyed by Guerrero and Margulis in their article in *The Sciences* cited in Chapter 3 notes.

Viruses, although they are capable of reproducing themselves, have no fueling or metabolizing equipment and instead depend on the living cells they invade (in most cases, bacteria or other single-cell organisms). This raises the question of how viruses could have originated. Although they are simpler than the simplest cells, they could not have been precursors of cellular life. Current theory is that viruses originated as detached, incomplete fragments of living cells. They are incredibly numerous. (Recent counts indicate about 10 million per milliliter in marine water, about 200,000 per milliliter in Texas drinking water, and about 2.5 billion per milliliter—the highest counts found thus far—in Canadian prairie wetlands.) Fortunately, relatively few varieties of viruses are harmful to life, and it is speculated that their peregrinations may even have significantly aided evolution by transporting small bits of DNA and RNA among organisms—as if they were genetic engineers. Cf., my speculation that rural pastoral and agricultural villages may have originated as detached, incomplete fragments of economically self-refueling settlements, much as most company towns originate today (p. 36 ff., *The Economy of Cities;* n. Ch. 3).

How Taiwan swiftly developed a versatile, expanding economy is described in my book *Cities and the Wealth of Nations: Principles of Economic Life* (New York: Random House, 1984, and Vintage, 1985).

The pet store in San Francisco was founded by Ansel Robison, who was a cousin of my grandfather; how it started comes from family lore; the bits about its later history are from a conversation in 1958 with the descendant of Ansel who then headed the company.

A means for countering some of the disadvantages of isolation to small entrepreneurs has been demonstrated by the Appalachian Center for Economic Networks, founded by June Holley in Athens, Ohio. It was described by Thomas Petzinger in his column "The Front Line," *The Wall Street Journal* (October 25, 1997). Networks of small, isolated enterprises—many, but not all, involving food production or processing—add value to each others' products with their own goods and services, as happens ordinarily within city economies but seldom among enterprises dispersed in small communities.

Cutting's enterprise, the Cutting Packing Co., was established in the 1870s. *Disturnell's Business Directory of California* (1882–83 edition) lists it under the classification "Hermetically sealed goods," at a Main Street location in San Francisco.

Japanese sewing machine manufacturers copied the efficient, earn-while-developing production methods pioneered in the late nineteenth century by Japanese bicycle manufacturers; described in *The Economy of Cities* (n. Ch. 3).

The anomalous expansion of the Los Angeles economy is described in "Undiscovered City," *Fortune* (June 1949). The anomalous shriveling of the Detroit supplier economy is discussed in "Paradox in Detroit," *Fortune* (January 1952).

If one city can feasibly produce (and perhaps export) specific goods or services, almost certainly other cities can, too. Thus, a major reason why cities lose export work is that other settlements replace it with their own production, either by new enterprises or by branch plants. Large and diverse city economies are particularly vulnerable to continual losses of older work from this cause because they have so many activities subject to import replacing elsewhere. If such a city seriously falters at replacing former imports (and generating new exports) on its own behalf, its economy does not merely stop growing; it dwindles and grows thin over time. This has happened in many an economically distressed city—for instance, Detroit and Buffalo. The complex repercussions of city import-replacing among cities, and also upon settlements and regions outside of cities, are discussed in *Cities and the Wealth of Nations* (n. this chapter).

Petzinger again, in his *Wall Street Journal* column (January 9 1998), notes that "new economies of locality are beginning to conquer old economies of scale," citing the fact that premium local beers, brewed in equipment occupying less than 100 square feet, "cost less than anything a giant factory can deliver." While this is one more new instance of the phenomenon, "economies of locality" are old; instances, continual. What's new, rather, is that business reporters and editors have begun noticing them.

5. EVADING COLLAPSE

Why "everything interesting happens at the edge of chaos" is succinctly put in "From Complexity to Perplexity," by John Horgan, *Scientific American* (June 1995): "[N]othing novel can emerge from systems with high degrees of order and stability, such as crystals. On the other hand, completely chaotic systems, such as turbulent fluids or heated gasses are *too* formless. Truly complex things—amoebae, bond traders and the like—appear at the border between rigid order and randomness." Horgan identifies "the edge of chaos" as most popular among thirty-one definitions of complexity compiled by Seth Lloyd, an MIT physicist. An overview of complexity and the fruitful, unstable borderland it occupies is set forth by Goerner in *Chaos and the Evolving Ecological Universe* (n. Ch. 3) and a subsequent book, *After the Clockwork Universe: The Emerging Science and Culture of Integral Society* (Edinburgh: Floris, 1999). Although these are decidedly not simplistic, people who aren't mathematicians can understand them.

The evolution of feet and body-supporting limbs was as necessary as lungs for permitting vertebrates to venture onto land; *National Geographic* on lungfish (May 1999). What could they eat in their novel habitat? Probably they were small and fueled themselves on insects that had preceded them on land; "Out of the Swamps," by Richard Monastersky, *Science News* (May 22, 1999). Insects required vegetation, which required land-dwelling bacteria: No development without co-development.

Single-cell organisms commonly benefit from crowding. Many species of bacteria engage in a communicating and organizing process called quorum sensing, meaning that individuals wait until they are numerous enough before spending energy to produce certain chemicals such as enzymes or luminescent molecules that are useful to them only in high concentrations; "Mob Action" by Evelyn Strauss, *Science News* (August 23, 1997). Quorum sensing implies that communication and coordination among independent, individual cells preceded the emergence of multicelled organisms.

Çatal Hüyük (also known as Çatalhöyük) is still being slowly and carefully excavated, but it is evident that in 7000 B.C., the settlement had a dense population of five to ten thousand people. Their abundant art strongly hints that their culture was not early Neolithic but derived in an unbroken line from the Paleolithic, the Old Stone Age. The site was discovered by James Mellaart in 1958; he excavated from 1961 until 1965, when, for mysterious reasons, he was banned by the Turkish government. After a lapse of thirty years, excavation resumed under direction of another English archaeologist, Ian Hodder. An account of the different scientific emphases and methods of the two archaeologists—owing to changes in archaeological techniques and interests in the meantime—is given in "A Tale of Two Obsessed Archaeologists . . ." by Robert Kunzig, *Discover* (May 1999). Domesticated sheep and goat bones are mingled with a high proportion of wild-game remains, and domesticated plant food with a high proportion of wild food. Çatal Hüyük was an older settlement than even the most ancient farming villages in its vicinity. I have speculated how such a center could develop and support itself before the dawn of agriculture and then later, when agriculture was merely a sideline, in *The Economy of Cities* (n. Ch. 3).

Economic failures can often live to try again and even become successes. A notable example, because his subsequent success was so spectacular, was Henry Ford, who failed with two tries at manufacturing automobiles before his third attempt succeeded. "The Flexible Tiger," *The Economist* (January 3, 1998), draws attention to frequent failures of Taiwanese companies and the ease with which their proprietors can start anew, and contrasts the stability of the Taiwanese economy with that of Asian countries where failed enterprises are kept on life support with unrepaid loans. The moral: Small-scale, rapid, responsive corrections benefit overall stability.

Forced birth control in China, mandating one child per couple, is intended to reduce population. It also carries other consequences, such as an imbalance of the sexes owing to preference for sons over daughters and, if it continues, the disappearance of extended families as aunts, uncles, and cousins vanish. Other probably unintended consequences for the society are unforeseeable.

The fog harvested by coast redwoods was measured by Todd Dawson of Cornell University and the University of California at Berkeley. His findings are described in "Clues to Redwoods' Mighty Growth Emerge in Fog," by Carol Kaesuk Yoon, *The New York Times* (November 24, 1998).

In sampled forest streams in the Pacific Northwest, the tissues of young salmon that have not yet migrated to sea contain an average of 40 percent of ocean-derived elements; salmonberry bushes at streamside derive 18 percent of their nitrogen from ocean sources; and some twenty forest vertebrates are partially nourished on ocean-derived nutrients. "The forest raises the salmon, but the salmon also raise the forest. . . . The fish leave the bay's web of streams no larger than a fat pencil and disappear into the ocean for three to six years. They return weighing up to sixty pounds, all biomass . . . harvested from the sea"; *The Forest That Fish Built,* by Richard Manning (Portland, Ore.: Ecotrust, 1996).

Norbert Wiener introduced his new word to the public in *Cybernetics, or Control and Communication in the Animal and the Machine* (New York: Wiley, 1949).

In 1976, when cod stocks off Newfoundland were already starting to decline, the Canadian government's so-called Dept. of the Environment declared in its *Policy for Canada's Commercial Fisheries* that fisheries management was to be guided not by "biological factors" but by economic and social issues, stating that in the past, fishing had been regulated in the interest of the fish but that "in the future it is to be regulated in the interest of the people who depend on the fishing industry." Since the complete collapse of cod stocks sixteen years later, and severe dwindling of other groundfish, fishermen have been encouraged to concentrate on species lower in marine food-webs, such as shrimp and crabs—in spite of warnings by scientists that overfishing of these species, which cod and other groundfish feed on, jeopardizes recovery of the depleted stocks. Newfoundland's fishing and processing communities now live on the many-fewer jobs—but higher-profit processing plants—provided by this second-tier version of overfishing. The other principal recourse has been emigration; between the collapse of the cod fishery in 1992 and 1998, net out-migration from the province roughly tripled from that of preceding years, to some fifty thousand persons, who were mostly workers under the age of thirty-five, creating a rising ratio of dependents to people of working age. So much for the Dept. of the Environment's fatuous assumption that biological factors can be separated from economic and social issues. "Cod Don't Vote," by Elizabeth Brubaker, *Next City* (Toronto: Winter 1998–99); "Down and Down in Newfoundland," by Jeffrey Simpson, *The Globe and Mail* (Toronto, November 10, 1998); "Keeping the Fish Plants Busy," by Don Cayo, *The Globe and Mail* (January 25, 1999).

Attempts to reason out causes of major climate changes and anticipate effects of global warming from greenhouse gases become extremely complicated when changes of ocean salinity owing to meltwater from ice and resulting shifts in ocean currents and wind temperatures are factored in. Lovelock, who considers that interglacial warm periods such as the present are "pathologies" of the earth, reasons that when large volumes of water are locked into northern and southern ocean and continental ice caps, potentially fertile continental shelves are uncovered, yielding more scope for life. He also reasons that cool ice ages beneficially counter slowly increasing heat from the sun; *The Ages of Gaia* (n. Ch. 3), p. 135 ff.

The U.S. government spends, or extends as special tax benefits, $21 billion annually to subsidize carbon dioxide–producing fossil fuels. This figure is from "A Good Climate for Investment," by Ross Gelbspan, in *The Atlantic Monthly* (June 1998). The good investments he refers to are in non-carbon-producing energy sources.

A two-income, two-child family in a Toronto suburb, with an income somewhat above average, supporting two cars (one three years old; the other, five), spends just about as much on the cars and their insurance, maintenance, gasoline, and parking per month as it is able to budget monthly for food, clothing, heating and other utilities, household upkeep and repairs, and recreation. "This family is one disaster away from losing their home." From a letter to the editor, "Why Ontario's working people voted for Tories," in the *Toronto Star* (June 12, 1999).

Codfishing subsidies in Canada swelled from 1981 on; boatbuilding, boat and fishing equipping, fish plants, and incomes of fishermen and plant workers were all subsidized. By 1990, two years before the fishery collapsed, Newfoundland fishermen were receiving $1.60 in benefits from the government for every $1 earned in the fishery. Other subsidies came to a roughly equal amount, in total reaching more than three times what the fishery earned. This is why, had it been possible to include subsidies in costs, cod would have been priced out of the market. Subsidy costs were calculated by economists at Newfoundland's Memorial University; "Cod Don't Vote," *Next City* (n. above).

Orexin was identified by a team led by Masashi Yanagisawa of the Howard Hughes Medical Institute, University of Texas Southwestern Medical Center. The researchers believe orexin is only one of several substances triggering desire to eat in response to low-energy blood levels. "Scientists Track Down Trigger for Hunger," by Carolyn Abraham, *The Globe and Mail* (Toronto, February 20, 1998). According to *The Skinny on Fat*, by Shawna Vogel (New York: Freeman, 1999), at least 130 different genes seem to take part in setting a person's weight.

Specialization at the expense of diversity is unwholesome for both economies and ecosystems. Uzbekistan affords an extreme illustration. As a Soviet republic, it was ordered to concentrate on growing cotton. To irrigate the crops, the Aral Sea, the world's fourth-largest lake, was reduced by half its surface area and its two rivers were erased, leaving vast areas of sand contaminated with pesticides, defoliants, salt, heavy metals, and sewage. This produces poisonous sand storms that reach as far as the Himalayas and contaminate not only Uzbekistan but Kazakhstan and Turkmenistan; they are afflicting Central Asians with appalling rates of tuberculosis, anemia, infant mortality, cancer, birth defects, and liver and kidney disorders. From a human point of view, Uzbekistan's horrors may represent the single most calamitous ecological breakdown of modern times. Post-Soviet Uzbekistan's government continues the policy of concentrating on cotton because, in this blighted land, there are now no alternatives left to depend upon for revenues. Foreign aid has been futile; "Uzbekistan, a Dying Lake, a Human Diet of Chalk," by Geoffrey York, *The Globe and Mail* (Toronto, November 22, 1997). Although this example of sacrifice to supposed efficiency of all-out specialization is extreme, the inability of economies specializing at the expense of ample diversity to find alternate work for themselves is not unusual. Yet Adam Smith's simplistic reasoning about the theoretical advantage of international division of labor to exploit comparative advantages (which are almost always temporary) is still amazingly influential. For example, here are words of wisdom written as recently as 1997 by an American billionaire philanthropist: "Global integration has brought . . . the benefits of the international division of labor, which are so clearly proved by the doctrine of comparative advantage . . ."

The example of tightly integrated feedback control in a termite colony is taken from *The Evolution of Complexity by Means of Natural Selection,* by John Tyler Bonner (Princeton, N.J.: Princeton University Press, 1988).

Russian economic disarray as the Soviet Union was breaking down politically is depicted in *Lenin's Tomb,* by David Remnick (New York: Random House, 1993). *The Economist* (April 24, 1999) sums up prospects a decade after the breakup: "Russia in 2000 will be one of a miserable clutch of countries where things look less hopeful than they did 100 years ago."

National currency feedback on international trade could improve because small nations are growing more numerous—but only if they have their own currencies. At present, the smallest nation with its own is Iceland (population 270,000). Small national size is no economic disadvantage. Of the world's ten nations with a population of more than 100 million, only the United States and Japan are well off economically. Of the ten most prosperous nations, the largest—apart from the United States and Japan—is Belgium (population 10,200,000); "Small but Perfectly Formed," *The Economist* (January 3, 1998).

Organisms' adaptations to freezing temperatures are complex and various; they include production of antifreeze chemicals, elimination from the body of materials that can trigger formation of ice crystals, increased blood-clotting capacity to protect capillaries from freezing, and ability to expel water from organs into noncellular body cavities; "Lifestyles of the Cold and Frozen," by Kenneth B. Storey and Janet M. Storey, *The Sciences* (New York Academy of Sciences, May/June 1999). Our own feedback regulations of body heat and our adaptations of clothing, shelter, and fireplaces and furnaces, while not as complex as what goes on in a cocoon, are pretty remarkable, too.

The initial fire in a forest typically does relatively little harm to tree trunks, protected as they are by bark. But a subsequent fire soon afterward can be devastating. Historically, the time elapsing between fires in tropical forests was four hundred years or more, but where settlers have moved in, accidental fires occur about every three years. Forest fires operate as vicious circles—two make another more likely, and so on, culminating in the dead end of the forest's loss; "Amazon Forests Caught in Fiery Feedback," by S. Milius, *Science News* (October 3, 1998).

6. THE DOUBLE NATURE OF FITNESS FOR SURVIVAL

The ways of bonobos are described and photographically illustrated in *Bonobo: The Forgotten Ape,* by Frans de Waal (Berkeley: University of California Press, 1997).

The selfish-gene theory was expounded by Richard Dawkins in *The Selfish Gene* (Oxford: Oxford University Press, 1976; second revised edition, 1989).

Darwin, in a letter to A. R. Wallace (1871), posed the puzzle of altruism thus: "He who was ready to sacrifice his life . . . rather than betray his comrades, would often leave no offspring to inherit his noble nature. The bravest men, who were always willing to come to the front in war, and who freely risked their lives for others, would on an average perish in larger numbers than other men." He then speculated that individual self-sacrifice can promote survival of the trait through natural selection because it is a valuable asset in military competition between tribes. But this still leaves the puzzle of how the trait can propagate if individuals carrying it disproportionately expunge themselves. The letter is quoted on p. 327 of *The Ant and the Peacock* (n. Ch. 2).

Our utilitarian sense of sight equips us for activities unnecessary to survival, such as designing cornices; manual dexterity permits us to play oboes; powers of observation permit us to navigate by the stars; ability to communicate permits us to teach arithmetic and stage pageants—all of which makes it hardly surprising that women's willingness to undergo childbirth repeatedly with dignity and self-esteem should also have equipped us (males as well as females) to endure self-sacrifice in warfare and fire fighting and to find gratification in giving our cloak to someone colder, our loaf to someone hungrier. The underlying principle—that the evolutionary legacy bursts "with potential along a thousand possible pathways"—is expounded by Stephen Jay Gould in a number of his interesting essays; for example, "The Great Seal Principle," in *Eight Little Piggies* (New York: Norton, 1993), from which the quotation about the multiple pathways is taken.

Similarities of human males and females permit cooperation in many activities, and also permit individuals of one gender to assume responsibilities of the other when necessary—a survival advantage to both individuals and their progeny, unavailable to mammals such as walruses and moose, whose genders lead relatively separate lives, or of course to creatures like spiders, whose males and females differ profoundly from each other.

Recent dating studies of wholesale extinctions of large mammals in Australia indicate that these coincided with arrival on the continent of Homo sapiens about fifty thousand years ago. But whether the extinctions resulted from overhunting or from habitat destruction by deliberately set fires is in dispute, according to *Science* (January 8, 1999). Wholesale extinctions of large animals in North America followed close upon an influx of human beings at the end of the last ice age, about eleven thousand years ago; *Science News* (January 9, 1999).

Marcus Gee, in "Richer Is Cleaner," *The Globe and Mail* (Toronto, December 10, 1997), draws attention to this impasse: When economies grow rich, they start cleaning up air pollution, but to reach that degree of wealth, they must first increase air pollution; he takes as his examples the increasing pollution from coal combustion in India and China. The moral he draws is that anything which slows economic growth in poor countries also retards environmental cleanup: "To put it crudely, poor countries must pollute today to clean up tomorrow. We in the rich world may not like it, but it's how we did it." One might add, however, that currently rich countries' automobiles are major contributors to global air pollution and that if rich countries proceed to develop energy from wind and solar power, these advances will also then be available to currently poor countries—much as burning coal instead of cow dung became available to India after England demonstrated that coal could be used as fuel instead of wood.

The book on symbioses between governments and economies to which Hiram refers is my book *Systems of Survival: Moral Foundations of Commerce and Politics* (New York: Random House, 1992, and Vintage, 1994). Frans de Waal argues in *Good Natured: The Origins of Right and Wrong in Humans and Other Animals* (Cambridge, Mass.: Harvard University Press, 1996) that members of species living successfully in social groups have developed practices and rules for dealing with internal competition. Now, here is another evolutionary puzzle: Cannibalism is conventionally seen to be rare among human beings because it is considered wrong, but it is quite as rare, or more so, among many other species of carnivores and omnivores, and this is strange at first thought, because to eat another member of the same species is obviously a first-class method of obtaining the most suitable nutrition and, simultaneously, of disposing of competitors. So why isn't cannibalism commonplace or even universal throughout nature? One answer, derived from a study of cannibalistic tiger salamanders, seems to be that the practice carries with it a high risk of disease, because "pathogens that target the dinner target the diner too"; "Why Aren't There More Cannibals Around?" by S. Milius, *Science News* (May 9, 1998). This vulnerability principle checks with the observation that cannibals in New Guinea fall prey to a fatal disease called kuru, which they acquire from eating the brains of their human dinners. Kuru is akin to mad cow disease, which is transmitted to cattle in feed containing offal from sheep afflicted with a brain disease called scrapie.

7. Unpredictability

A short history of how science has dealt with three great classes of problems—simplicity, disorganized complexity, and organized complexity—drawing heavily upon an essay by Dr. Warren Weaver in an *Annual Report of the Rockefeller Foundation* (New York, 1958) can be found in the last chapter of my book *The Death and Life of Great American Cities* (New York: Random House, 1961).

The "butterfly effect" derives from the title of a paper that Edward Lorenz presented at a meeting of the American Association for the Advancement of Science in Washington, D.C., on December 29, 1972: "Predictability: Does the Flap of a Butterfly's Wings in Brazil Set Off a Tornado in Texas?" The question, as he immediately went on to explain, is unanswerable but reaches into the core of weather's nature—its inherent instability. Although the paper was not published except as a press release of the conference, the ideas it expressed, and the experimentation behind them, gained wide currency among chaos theorists (and other scientists) in the years following. In 1990, Lorenz prepared three lectures for delivery at the University of Washington, describing the chaotic behavior of weather patterns and their relationship to other chaos phenomena. (To chaos theorists, *chaos* does not carry its popular meaning of an utter mess; while it involves randomness, it has its laws, which the theorists usually present mathematically or diagrammatically.) Lorenz's three university lectures, along with first publication of the famous 1972 butterfly paper, are available in *The Essence of Chaos*, by Lorenz (Seattle: University of Washington Press, 1993).

An ecosystem is not equipped to control itself by command or other centralized arrangement, because it lacks a command post—a central nervous system or its equivalent. Its means of adjustment, change, and organization consist of actions and interactions within and among the organisms comprising it. *The*

Beak of the Finch: A Story of Evolution in Our Time, by Jonathan Weiner (New York: Knopf, 1994, and Vintage, 1995), describes concretely how a specific ecosystem on a Galápagos island makes itself up as it goes along, shaped by happenstance events and its organisms' adjustments to them.

Unpredictability implies both welcome and unwelcome surprises. A person's general attitude toward uncertainty probably depends on temperament, upbringing, experience, and external circumstances. It seems that many people—perhaps most—crave predictability: witness the popularity of astrology, omens, prophecies, science fiction, weather almanacs, and economic forecasts. To recoil from the concept that the world unpredictably makes itself up without purpose, plan, or planner puts us in sympathetic touch with ancestors disturbed by tidings that the earth is not flat but round, that it spins unsupported in space, that it is not at the center of the solar system, much less of all the heavens.

Even such an important and well-assimilated bifurcation as use of electric power for industrial purposes started out modestly and only gradually worked its way into economies, in America taking forty years after the introduction of the electric dynamo to account for 50 percent of the power used in industrial production. During twenty years when its use was increasing from 5 to 50 percent of U.S. industrial power, growth of productivity in the country's industry actually declined. *The Economist* (September 28, 1996) drew a parallel to forty years of gradual growth of computers in industry, accompanied by lack of productivity growth attributable to computers. It quoted Robert Solow, a Nobel Prize–winning economist, that "you can see computers everywhere but in the productivity statistics."

The trade journal with the plastics-denigrating technical editor (who was one of my bosses at the time) was *The Iron Age*. His candidate for the wonder material of the near future was titanium.

In 1998 the world's fastest-growing source of electric energy was wind power, having quadrupled its production in the preceding ten years. However, since that expansion started from a minuscule base, it still accounted for only about 7 percent of electric generation even in Denmark, the world's leading producer, where hundreds of small cooperatives with some one hundred thousand shareholders run wind turbines. However, in some regions of Europe, wind generation has become as cheap as or cheaper than coal-fired generation. In California, the leading generator of wind power in the United States, production throughout the state amounts to the equivalent of the power used in San Francisco. Montana and Texas are catching up with California. The world's leading manufacturers of wind-power equipment are, not surprisingly, in Denmark, California, and the state of Washington. "It's Blowin' in the Wind Power," by Dan Falk, *The Globe and Mail* (Toronto, September 5, 1998). Proponents of clean and renewable-resource energy do not want to see attempts to develop solar- and geothermal-power generation neglected, reasoning that a mix of methods is always more flexible than concentration on a single technology.

In China, where it takes up to a month to clear a check because of inefficiency of the formal banking system, businesses have self-organized a parallel banking system. Although it is illegal there to use credit cards for credit, it is not illegal to make deposits into a credit card account and then draw on those deposits to make payments. Owing to this novel use of credit cards for large transactions among businesses, the second-largest market of MasterCard—surpassed only by the U.S. market—is China; turnover is $73 billion annually. The advantage is MasterCard's efficiency; it verifies business funds on hand without delay and transfers them immediately. The formal banking system is struggling to become efficient enough to compete with the self-organized system; *The Economist* (January 2, 1999).

I was shown the Hong Kong jade market and the nearby jade traders by Mel Manchester. We disagree about the age of the traders who were setting global prices. He says they included men of all ages; to me, they all looked surprisingly young.

Many organizations nowadays are consciously trying to figure out how they can use self-organizing principles without becoming either disintegrated or inert—in short, as avatars of fruitful complexity. Ecotrust lists these three requirements: (a) autonomous agents able to make independent decisions within a framework of relatively simple rules; (b) moderately dense network and web connections among the agents—that is, the organization's parts; and (c) vigorous experimentation by agents, disciplined by responding to feedback on results; *Draft Report on Operating Principles* (Portland, Ore.: Ecotrust, Oct. 1997). Much these same principles turn up in self-organizing groups as diverse as a successful neighborhood organization, credit card systems, and debugging and refinements contributed by users to Eric S. Raymond, a computer software designer, who shares his experience on the Web, at http://www.tuxedo.org/~esr/writings/cathedral-bazaar/. The part that takes hard thinking is the framework of underlying rules. They are crucial but must be as few as possible. The neighborhood organization referred to, which has remained strong, active, and productive for forty years, has only two rules: (a) any individual living or working in the area can become a member—no membership dues or other qualifications required—and can initiate undertakings or join with others; (b) no undertaking can displace any person or business in the area.

8. ARMBRUSTER'S PROMISE

Phillip McCrory, of Huntsville, Alabama, is the hairdresser. The first use of his invention was to mop up an accidental spill of diesel oil in a ditch of water at NASA's Marshall Space Flight Center, for which McCrory devised a rough filter consisting of seven kilos of hair clippings in a barrel. After filtering, the water contained only seventeen parts per million of oil. Hair shafts are covered with minute cuticles that attract and hold oil. "What to Do About Oil Spills? Ask a Hairdresser," by Claudia Dreifus, *The New York Times*, reprinted in *The Globe and Mail* (Toronto, June 20, 1998). Many years ago, an oil spill off the east coast of Canada was successfully mopped up with peat moss, but nothing further came of this because of the impractical bulkiness of peat moss. I am indebted for this information to Dr. Ursula Franklin, emeritus professor of materials science, University of Toronto.

Acknowledgments

The chief co-developer of this book is my editor and publisher, Jason Epstein, whose questions, criticisms, advice, and uncanny perception of what I was trying to do have been integral to the book's evolution from early, groping drafts to its completion. Other major co-developers are my three children, Dr. James K. Jacobs, Edward D. Jacobs, and Burgin (Mary H.) Jacobs, to whom this book is dedicated. Their unstinted sharing of knowledge, suggestions for reading, ideas, wit, thoughtfulness, and good spirits have been immeasurably helpful not only to me but also directly to the book.

I'm grateful to many other relatives, friends, and strangers, who have supplied useful materials, background information, criticism, or other assistance. They include: Sid Adilman, Toshiko Adilman, Max Allen, Richard Anderson, Spencer B. Beebe, Lincoln Bergman, Alan Broadbent, Patricia Broms, Dr. Decker Butzner, John Cleveland, Mary Ann Code, Dr. Ursula Franklin, Dr. Sally Goerner, Dr. Lucia F. Jacobs, Richard C. Keeley, Dr. Marvin Lunenfeld, Mel Manchester, Alana Probst, Mary Rowe, Dr. Stan Rowe, and Jane Zeidler; also my editor and publisher at Modern Library, David Ebershoff; my copy editor, Veronica Windholz; my editor at Random House of Canada, Anne Collins; Ulf Buchholz; and again Edward Jacobs, who compiled the index.

The chief substantive generalities from which this book emerged are evolutionary theory and economic history; its form emerged from the literary tradition of didactic dialogue. Therefore, only the preceding work of many thousands of co-developers, most of them no longer living and most, by far, unknown to me even by name, has made possible the specific developmental differentiation that this book represents. A few are mentioned in the text or notes. I am deeply indebted to them all and grateful for their work, without which this book would have nothing to say.

Index

ALSO BY JANE JACOBS

THE DEATH AND LIFE OF GREAT AMERICAN CITIES

A classic since its publication in 1961, this book is the definitive
statement on American cities: what makes them safe, how they
function, and why all too many official attempts at saving them
have failed. Jacobs, writing on architecture in New York City in
the early sixties, argued that urban diversity and vitality were
being destroyed by powerful architects and city planners.
Rigorous, sane, and delightfully epigrammatic, Jacobs's small
masterpiece is a blueprint for the judicious management of cities.
Thirty years later, it is still sensible, knowledgeable, and indispensable.

*"Perhaps the most influential single work in the history
of town planning."* —The New York Times

Sociology/0-679-74195-X

SYSTEMS OF SURVIVAL

A Dialogue on the Moral Foundations of Commerce and Politics

With the same far-ranging intelligence and clarity of observation
that she brought to her classic works on cities, Jacobs addresses
the moral values that underpin all of public life. She takes a
shrewd look at business fraud and criminal enterprise, overex-
tended government farm subsidies, and zealous transit police to
show what happens when the moral systems of commerce collide
with those of politics.

Sociology/0-679-74816-4

Also available:

Cities and the Wealth of Nations, 0-394-72911-0

The Economy of Cities, 0-394-70584-X

VINTAGE BOOKS
Available at your local bookstore, or call toll-free to order:
1-800-793-2665 (credit cards only).